# SWIFT'S CLASSICAL RHETORIC

UNIVERSITY OF GEORGIA MONOGRAPHS, NO. 8

71251

# Swift's
# Classical
# Rhetoric

By
CHARLES ALLEN BEAUMONT

DEPARTMENT OF ENGLISH
UNIVERSITY OF GEORGIA

UNIVERSITY OF GEORGIA PRESS
ATHENS                    1961

For My Mother and Father

# Contents

PREFACE                                                        vii

I   SWIFT'S CRITICAL COMMENTS UPON RHETORIC                      1

II  "A MODEST PROPOSAL"                                         15

III "AN ARGUMENT AGAINST ABOLISHING CHRISTIANITY"              44

IV  "A VINDICATION OF LORD CARTERET"                           87

V   "THE ANSWER TO THE CRAFTSMAN"                             119

VI  RECURRING RHETORICAL PATTERNS                             138

    NOTES                                                     149

    GLOSSARY                                                  155

    INDEX                                                     158

# Preface

GREAT satire can hardly exist without the devices of rhetoric. Jonathan Swift relied almost exclusively upon classical rhetoric as a means of creating the ironies of his essays of total ironic inversion. The aim of the present study is to explore Swift's method in using the varied devices of classical rhetoric to create, sustain, and render plausible the ironic norms of these essays. Swift has used some of the devices without alteration from their ancient form; others he has refined into subtler functions. Through classical rhetoric, he has succeeded in casting over these essays an illusion of tight and irrefutable argument and an illusion that his author's point of view is somehow inevitably right. Indeed, some readers have been so impressed with Swift's elaborate and complex use of classical rhetoric they feel that the constant and sometimes electric play of this rhetoric is almost infinite. This present exploration will seek to render finite Swift's use of classical rhetoric and to examine in detail its functioning in the ironical essays.

For the ironical essays I have used the texts edited by Professor Herbert Davis (aided by Professor Louis A. Landa), without whose careful scholarship no such close textual study as the present one could be done in America. For Swift's letters, I have used Professor F. E. Ball's edition of the *Correspondence*. And for *A Tale of a Tub*, I have used the text prepared by A. C. Guthkelch and D. Nichol Smith.

Athens, Georgia                                                              C.A.B.

## CHAPTER I

# Swift's Critical Comments Upon Rhetoric

AT Kilkenny School and at Trinity College, Dublin, Swift was trained in classical rhetoric, not only in specific courses in rhetoric but also in a program of instruction which was fundamentally based upon the rhetorical methods of composition and public and private debate *pro forma*.[1] Fortunately Swift does not leave us to speculate on how much of this training he absorbed; he has been quite vocal on the subject of rhetoric in *A Tale of a Tub*, the *Journal to Stella*, some of the essays, and some of the sermons.

The richest single work on the subject is *A Tale of a Tub*, in which is reflected his intimate knowledge of rhetoric as an art, of orators, and of the jargon of rhetorical handbooks and treatises.

The Author refers several times to the commonplaces of panegyric. In the Dedication to Lord Somers, the Author's statement reflects two of these major commonplaces (public life and private life, with their several subdivisions) where arguments can be discovered. In classical rhetoric there are not "forty" or more, as the Author says, but he is satirizing specific examples of the commonplaces of panegyric, which are so common that they can be made to describe almost any man in Lord Somers' social and political station:

I expected, indeed, to have heard of your Lordship's Bravery, at the Head of an Army; Of your undaunted Courage, in mounting a Breach, or scaling a Wall; Or, to have had your Pedigree trac'd in a Lineal Descent from the House of *Austria*; Or, of your wonderful Talent at Dress and Dancing; Or, your Profound Knowledge in *Algebra*, *Metaphysicks*, and the Oriental Tongues. But to ply the World with an old beaten Story of your Wit, and Eloquence, and Learning, and Wisdom, and Justice, and

1

Politeness, and Candor, and Evenness of Temper in all Scenes of Life; Of that great Discernment in Discovering, and Readiness in Favouring deserving Men; with forty other common Topicks: I confess, I have neither Conscience, nor Countenance to do it. Because, there is no Virtue, either of a Public or Private Life, which some Circumstances of your own, have not often produced upon the Stage of the World; And those few, which for want of Occasions to exert them, might otherwise have pass'd unseen or unobserved by your *Friends*, your *Enemies* have at length brought to light.

In this passage we find the technique which Swift repeatedly uses in the *Tale*: at the same time that he is attacking bad rhetoric, he is giving an example of good rhetoric. The Dedication is good praise of Lord Somers, couched in the very rhetoric which Swift is attacking.

In the Preface the Author complains that the nature of man unduly limits the writer of panegyrics as to the number of commonplaces, for although the virtues of mankind can be counted on a few fingers, the vices and follies daily multiply. So, the writer must seek variety only in his words, since we have at hand only the few old virtues (and their related commonplaces) to work with. In an ironical statement, he praises these few virtues and commonplaces:

There is a Problem in an ancient Author, why Dedications, and other bundles of Flattery run all upon stale musty Topicks, without the smallest Tincture of any thing new; not only to the torment and nauseating of the *Christian* Reader, but (if not suddenly prevented) to the universal spreading of that pestilent Disease, the Lethargy, in this Island; whereas, there is very little Satyr which has not something in it untouch'd before. The Defects of the former Age are usually imputed to the want of Invention among those who are Dealers in that kind [panegyric]. . . .

The Author concludes that no "Art" of panegyric is sufficient unto itself, for "there is no inventing Terms of Art beyond our Idea's; and when Idea's are exhausted, Terms of Art must be so too." However, in England the problem is not important, because all Englishmen prefer satire, supposing it always to apply to the other fellow; but they hate panegyric unless it applies to themselves.

We have seen Swift's own brand of panegyric in the Dedication; he gives us another example of this art in the "Digression Concerning Critics." The Author writes that ". . . these *Antients*, highly sensible of their many Imperfections, must needs have endeavoured from some Passages of their works, to obviate, soften, or divert the Censorious Reader, by *Satyr*, or *Panegyrick* upon the *True Criticks*, in Imitation of their *Masters* the *Moderns*. Now, in the *Common-places* of both these, I was plentifully instructed, by a long Course of useful Study in *Prefaces* and *Prologues*." After so instructing himself in the manipulation of these commonplaces, the Author tries his own hand. His Panegyric on the True Critic is divided into two sections, the first being an investigation of the darkly couched fables of ancient writers about critics and the second being the Author's deduction about the critic based upon his observations of contemporary critics.[2]

The long Medieval and Renaissance debate over the proper roles of rhetoric and dialectic, and over whether all argument should be referred to dialectic or whether indemonstrable and improbable matters should be referred to rhetoric is not crucial in reference to Swift. However, from Plato forward, one can trace the argument that rhetoric is not an "Art" because it has no subject matter of its own. Swift in Section II of the *Tale* indicates his position on the matter and his opinion of the extremes to which a syllogism can be pushed. The brothers have just learned of the high fashion of gold lace and wish to place some on their coats. (Swift's footnote suggests that the Gold Lace stands for "the new Methods of forcing and perverting Scripture.") The brothers cannot find any authorization of the lace in the Will. But Peter, in a marvelous bit of argumentation, in a jumble of English and Latin, gets around this minor obstacle.

But about this time it fell out, that the Learned Brother aforesaid had read *Aristotelis Dialectica*, and especially that wonderful Piece *de Interpretatione*, which has the Faculty of teaching its Readers to find out a Meaning in every Thing but it self . . . .

Then the Learned Brother makes the inevitable rhetorical Division: wills are of two kinds; this will is of the second kind; the second kind is defined as, etc.

Brothers, he said, You are to be informed, that Wills, *duo sunt genera Nuncupatory* and *scriptory*: that in the Scriptory Will here before us, there is no Precept or Mention about Gold Lace, *conceditur*: But, *si idem affirmetur de nuncupatorio, negatur*, For Brothers, if you remember, we heard a Fellow say when we were Boys, that he heard my Father's Man say, that he heard my Father say, that he would advise his Sons to get Gold Lace on their Coats, as soon as ever they could procure money to buy it. By G____ that is very true, cries the other; I remember it perfectly well, said the third. And so without more ado they got the largest Gold Lace in the Parish, and walk'd about as fine as Lords.

This rhetorical principle of Division comes in for another attack in the Introduction. To show that rhetorical division can frequently be artificial and therefore foolishly limiting, the Author explains that because he is so enamoured of the number three, he will use that division, even though common sense would require a different division. (In setting up his kinds of oratory, he really needs a fourth division devoted to forensic oratory.)

. . . the Admission of them [lawyers] would overthrow a Number which I was resolved to establish, whatever Argument it might cost me; in imitation of that prudent Method observed by many other Philosophers and great Clerks, whose chief Art in Division has been, to grow fond of some proper mystical Number, which their Imaginations have rendered Sacred, to a Degree, that they force common Reason to find room for it in every part of Nature; reducing, including, and adjusting every Genus and Species within that Compass, by coupling some against their Wills, and banishing others at any Rate.

He then proceeds to proclaim the victory of having persuaded many who formerly adored the numbers 7 and *9* to shift their favor to the number *3*. He promises us again that he will publish a Panegyric on the Number Three. The Author thus explains why he must leave legal pleading out of his categories of Oratorical Machines. Swift implies the same argument to indicate a basic fault in allegory itself—at least in rigid, point-for-point allegory. Midway of the *Tale* he seems to need to introduce a fourth brother to represent a Church of England man, but he tells us that he is too attached to the number *3* to alter his allegory. Therefore, the reader must fend for himself in deciding when Martin is a Lutheran and when Martin is a Church of England man.

On the matter of decorating one's arguments with elaborate tropes and figures, Swift firmly declares himself for the "plain style" or for the judicious use of troping.[3] In addition to the basic attack on allegory implicit in the whole *Tale*, Swift gives us some specific examples of the piling up of metaphors. In the following example, he makes them the worse by yoking overly-homely or mean things to wisdom. The quotation is lengthy because the length is part of the point. He complains that writers of the present age have encouraged a superficial kind of reader because they do not encourage the reader to dig below the rind of things and pick the meaning out:

whereas, Wisdom is a Fox, who after long hunting, will at last cost you the Pains to dig out: 'Tis a Cheese, which by how much the richer, has the thicker, homelier, and the courser Coat; and whereof to a judicious Pa[la]te, the Maggots are the best. 'Tis a Sack-Posset, wherein the deeper you go, you will find it the sweeter. Wisdom is a Hen, whose Cackling we must value and consider, because it is attended with an Egg; But then, lastly, 'tis a Nut, which unless you chuse with judgment, may cost you a Tooth, and pay you nothing but a Worm. In consequence of these momentous Truths, the Grubaean Sages have always chosen to convey their Precepts and their Arts, shut up within the Vehicles of Types and Fables, which having been perhaps more careful and curious in adorning, than was altogether necessary, it has fared with these Vehicles after the usual Fate of Coaches over-finely painted and gilt; that the transitory Gazers have so dazzled their Eyes, and fill'd their Imaginations with the outward Lustre, as neither to regard or consider, the Person or the Parts of the Owner within. A Misfortune we undergo with somewhat less Reluctancy, because it has been common to us with Pythagoras, Aesop, Socrates, and other of our Predecessors.

By no stretch of the imagination are these Greeks, who *knew* how to communicate through the well-chosen figure, "predecessors" of the Grub Street tropers in any sense of the word except its completely literal sense.

One more example of this overuse of figure will suffice here. In Section VI, Jack and Martin have been removing the ornaments from their coats, Martin in an orderly way and Jack with such zeal that his coat is in shreds,

So that he [Jack] looked like a drunken Beau, half rifled by Bullies; Or like a fresh Tenant of Newgate, when he refused the Payment of a Garnish; Or like a discovered Shoplifter, left to the Mercy of Exchange-Women; Or like a Bawd in her old Velvet-Petticoat, resign'd into the secular Hands of the Mobile. Like any, or like all of these, a Meddley of Rags, and Lace, and Rents, and Fringes, unfortunate Jack did now appear.

The reiteration of *or*, plus "like any, or like all," further emphasizes Swift's distaste for overuse of simile.

Not content with merely expository attacks upon hollow eloquence and peculiar reasoning techniques, Swift, in Section XI of the *Tale*, gives us an actual sample of Jack's "Great eloquence, and the Force of his Reasoning upon such Abstruse Matters" as preordination. The passage is much too long to quote here, but we can summarize it and conclude with its last rolling sentence. Jack explains that his nose has hit a Lamp-post, as was ordained some few days before creation, and that there is nothing uncommon in this collision, for how many more misadventures do we run into with our eyes wide open. The inward eye is a better light for our guidance than the outer eye; *ergo*, it is better to walk in the dark.

For, O ye Eyes, Ye blind Guides; miserable Guardians are Ye of our Noses; Ye, I say, who fasten upon the first Precipice in view, and then tow our wretched willing Bodies after You, to the very Brink of Destruction: But, alas, that Brink is rotten, our Feet slip, and we tumble down prone into a Gulph, without one hospitable Shrub in the Way to break the Fall; a Fall, to which not any Nose of mortal Make is equal, except that of the Giant Lauralco, who was Lord of the Silver Bridge. Most properly, therefore, O Eyes, and with great Justice, may You be compared to those foolish Lights, which conduct Men thro' Dirt and Darkness, till they fall into a deep Pit, or a noisom Bog.

These are the main passages from the *Tale* which indicate Swift's close knowledge of and abiding interest in rhetoric, but before leaving this topic, we should take particular note of an important critical essay by Professor Harold D. Kelling, who suggests that the real subject of the whole *Tale of a Tub* volume is rhetoric: most of the work is examples of delusive rhetoric, and some of the passages contain either explicit or implicit examples of or comments upon good rhetoric.[4]

Professor Kelling begins by noting that the whole work

is in the form of a classical oration: the prefatory material is an elaborate *exordium;* the narration (reasons for writing) is the Preface; the first paragraph of the Introduction contains the subject and its definition (panegyric rhetoric which is over the heads of the audience); in the second paragraph of the Introduction comes the Division. Swift's lumping his three sections of his Division into one—delusive oratory—indicates the unity of his subject; that is, the oratory of pulpit, of learned writers, and of Grub Street writing has delusive rhetoric in common. The subject of the whole work, then, is delusive rhetoric and its opposite, and the two ostensible topics (religion and learned authors) merely offer material whose rhetoric is to be criticized. The "Mechanical Operation of the Spirit," far from being merely a brilliant appendage to the work, is literally the "moving" peroration to the whole. The main value of demonstrating that the whole work is a five-part classical speech is to indicate the unity of all the parts, and especially of the fifth part.

The heart of Professor Kelling's argument is that the Modern Author of the *Tale* is himself using delusive rhetoric, the kind of rhetoric which Swift is attacking. Swift repeatedly allows his Modern Author to work himself into ridiculous argumentative positions and conclusions. Kelling's point is that Swift depends upon the careful reader to perceive how unreasonable the Modern Author is and to deduce for himself the proper conclusion. Thus the perceptive reading of the *Tale* completes Swift's instructing the reader about what good rhetoric is by giving him examples of delusive rhetoric. (By "good rhetoric" Kelling means writing based upon competent use of rhetorical argument which tends to *show* to the audience what is reasonable; by "delusive or bad rhetoric" is meant an extreme appeal to the emotions through illegitimate use of rhetorical argument or through a complete abandonment of any semblance of reasonable argument.) Kelling feels that Swift makes the false rhetoric of the Modern Author so extreme and so obvious that the reader is forced to see the error. "In effect," Kelling states,

The *Tale of a Tub* is a dialogue between two kinds of delusive orators, both contained within the schizoid modern author; the one, the author as he sees himself, uses abstractions and obscurity, finds everything good, and warns us against those who would strip off the fair exterior; the other, the modern as he is unconsciously, uses particulars which reveal rottenness everywhere and is thus a vitriolic satirist. But Swift is neither naive panegyrist nor bitter cynic and he is not trying to force his opinions upon the sane reader.

In the "Digression Concerning Critics," the Modern Author praises the True Critic for collecting authors' faults, and the Modern Author unconsciously reveals his cynicism by calling critics asses without horns, snarling dogs, etc. However, Swift also includes the critical norm in this speech by indicating that critics deduce rules for good writing which they arrive at by observing good writers and that they are restorers of old manuscripts. Kelling concludes,

The reasonable reader can accept this definition because such a critic allows him to use his own judgment, and he can see, furthermore, that Swift is this kind of critic in the *Tale*. Swift is drawing up rules by illustrating the principles of rational rhetoric that particulars communicate more clearly than generals, that references to common sense experience give a reader a chance to use his own reason, and the author's attitude should not be imposed upon the reader. The modern author as unconscious satirist is a rational orator in his use of particular references to common sense experience, but he mistakes his mad and rotten world for the normal and natural world. Swift appeals to reason because he compels the reader to see that the modern author has gone too far and stimulates the reader's normal and natural responses.

According to Kelling, then, Swift uses delusive rhetoric itself to force the reader to perceive by his own reasoning what delusive rhetoric is, and what good rhetoric is.

It is not necessary to accept Professor Kelling's reading to see the abundance of Swift's critical comments on rhetoric. Further observations of Swift concerning rhetoric can be found in his letters and in some of the essays and sermons.

Swift drew a sharp distinction between the elaborate rhetoric and irony of his satires and the clear, lucid exposition of his sermons. In Letter XI of the *Journal to Stella*, he states that

Mr. Harley and Mr. St. John are resolved that I must preach

before the Queen, and the Secretary of State has told me that he
will give me three weeks warning, but I desired to be excused.
. . . I hope they will forget it; for, if it should happen, all the
puppies hereabouts will throng to hear me, and expect something
wonderful, and be plaguily balked, for I shall preach plain honest
stuff.

A footnote in the original edition states that "the ministry
could never prevail upon the Doctor to preach before the
Queen." In much the same fashion Swift attacks wit and
troping in sermons in "A Letter to a Young Gentleman, Lately
Enter'd Holy Orders"; the young man should avoid such wit

Because, by the strictist Computation, it is very near a Million
to One, that you have none [wit]; and because too many
of your Calling, have consequently made themselves everlastingly
ridiculous by attempting it. I remember several young Men in this
Town, who could never leave the *Pulpit* under half a Dozen
*Conceits;* and this Faculty adhered to those Gentlemen a longer
or shorter time, exactly in Proportion to their several Degrees
of Dulness: Accordingly, I am told that some of them retain
it to this Day. I heartily wish the Brood were at an End.

This letter to the young priest might well be called a little
"Ars Rhetorica," for in it Swift treats of style, sources of
subject matter, some methods of persuasion, and delivery. He
begins by lamenting preachers' lack of study of the English
language and of their not even being aware of their poor
English style. Here he gives his famous definition of a good
prose style: "Proper Words in Proper Places." He urges the
young man to avoid the following stylistic faults. He should
avoid obscure terms—this includes "hard words" in general as
well as theological and philosophical jargon of the schools.
As Swift humorously comments, any "common Farmer shall
make you understand in three Words, that his *foot is out of
Joint*" whereas "a *Surgeon,* after a hundred terms of Art, if you
are not a Scholar, shall leave you to seek."[5] However, being a
good rhetorician, Swift adds that sermons preached before
special congregations should be adjusted to the specific listeners.
But the good preacher should always avoid the florid style of
rounded periods and grand cadences: "I have listened with my
utmost Attention for half an Hour to an Orator of this
Species, without being able to understand, much less to carry
away one single Sentence out of the whole Sermon."

Swift warns against "the Frequency of flat, unnecessary Epithets" and "the Folly of using old thread-bare Phrases" which are "nauseous to rational Hearers" and which seldom express one's meaning as well as "your own natural Words."[6]

Concurring in the Anglican contention that elaborate troping indicates cloudy thinking, Swift states

When a Man's Thoughts are clear, the properest Words will generally offer themselves first; and his own Judgment will direct him in what Order to place them, so they may be best understood. Where Men err against this Method, it is usually on Purpose, and to shew their Learning, their Oratory, their Politeness, or their Knowledge of the World. In short, that Simplicity, without which no human Performance can arrive to any great Perfection, is no where more eminently useful than in this.

Moving on from the subject of style, Swift considers "that Part of Oratory, which relates to the moving of the Passions." He states that some Anglicans and "all the Preachers and hearers of the *Fanatick* and *Enthusiastick* Strain" regularly make a strong play on the emotions. The young man, while studying Demosthenes and Cicero ("the two great Orators of *Greece* and *Rome*"), should remember that these men were frequently compelled to appeal to the audience's emotions "to enflame, or cool the Passions; especially at *Rome*, where *Tully* spoke" because these orators had to effect immediate action. The men they addressed were actually on the point either of acting or of avoiding action.[7] But a preacher is not aiming at immediate action based upon a temporary persuasion; he must appeal primarily to the hearer's reason so that the listener will sustain his acceptance for a whole life-time. There is nothing temporary in convincing a man how best to live his whole life. Even if this were not true, Swift gibes, emotional oratory "requires so much Art and Genius to arrive at any Perfection in it; as every Man will find, much sooner than learn, by consulting *Cicero* himself."

But Swift does not eschew all appeal to emotions, even in the plain style of the sermon, for he tells the young man,

If your Arguments be strong, in God's Name offer them in as moving a Manner as the Nature of the Subject will properly admit; wherein Reason, and good Advice will be your safest Guides: But beware of letting the pathetick Part swallow up the rational: For, I suppose, *Philosophers* have long agreed, that Passion should never prevail over Reason.

Swift states that the "Topicks" are from two sources: Scripture and Reason. The Scripture is used "to instruct the Hearers in the Limits, Extent, and Compass of every Duty," and reason is used to convince the hearers what their duty is and to convince them that they should do their duty. The sermon should be separated into as few "Divisions" as possible, and the "Heads of your Divisions" should be expressed in the fewest and simplest words possible. Swift follows this precept to the letter in his own sermons: the opening sentences or paragraphs are always succinct statements of the theme, and his transitions from the several divisions are heavily marked.[8]

Echoing the ancient plea of St. Augustine, Swift urges the young man seeking matter for his sermons, to avoid "the common unsufferable Cant" of disparaging "Heathen *Philosophers*" without first seeing what "those *Philosophers* can say for themselves." It is, for example, a "gross Piece of Ignorance" not to see that the moral part of Christianity is well expressed by Greek philosophers. Has not "that divine Precept of loving our Enemies" been expressed with convincing force by Plato?

Neither should the young cleric study too little "the principal Orators and Historians, and perhaps a few of the Poets" of antiquity. But, such study is for his general education, not for spattering his sermons with quotations. Even quotations from the Bible should be sparingly used. Quotations from ancient Fathers and learned Prelates should be used mainly to confirm controverted points.

A Christian preacher should never place himself in the dilemma of trying to explain the Christian Mysteries, for obviously if they are Mysteries, they are inexplicable. Neither should he be at pains to follow the common practice of attacking atheism, deism, free-thinking, and the like.

Swift recommends the rhetorical device of appeal to self-interest if the appeal to the hearer's natural reason fails, for "*Reasoning* will never make a Man correct an ill Opinion, which by *Reasoning* he never acquired . . . ." To convince such a man to behave properly "is no easy Task." However, "if you could once convince the Town or Country Profligate, by Topicks drawn from the View of their own Quiet, Reputation, Health, and Advantage; their Infidelity would soon drop off . . . ."

Swift also instructs the young priest in oratorical delivery. He should deliver the sermon without reading it, unless he can perfect the trick of reading without appearing to be reading. He should never let his head bob up and down from his paper to his listeners "like an idle School-Boy on a Repetition-Day." The preacher should compose his sermon far enough in advance to allow about two days of practice in delivery: "To which you will probably answer some Years hence, *That it was just finished when the last Bell rang to Church*; and I shall readily believe, but not excuse you."

Swift concludes his "Art of Rhetoric" by promising the young man that he will also write him a brief treatise on moral character necessary to the priest.

Swift's exacting knowledge of the art of rhetoric is reflected in his delightful "Letter of Thanks from My Lord W[harton] to the Lord Bishop of S. Asaph, In the Name of the Kit-Cat-Club." Bishop Fleetwood had published four sermons, with a preface, on the revolution settlement. The Whigs snapped this book up for widespread circulation because of its extremely liberal point of view toward the settlement. Swift, wishing to attack the Bishop's opinion and, especially wishing to attack the use to which Wharton and the other Whigs had put these sermons, contrived this pretended letter. The Bishop was given to a florid style of preaching; and, after Swift has Wharton praise the political implications of the sermons, he turns to praise the rhetorical heights of the Preface:

Here your Lordship rises, if possible, above yourself: Never was such Strength of Thought, Such Beauty of Expression, so happily joined together. Heavens! Such Force, such Energy in each pregnant Word! Such Fire, Such Fervour, in each glowing Line! . . . . Who can read, unmov'd, these following Strokes of Oratory? "Such was the Fame, Such was the Reputation, Such was the Faithfulness and Zeal, to Such a Height of Military Glory, Such was the Harmony and Consent, Such was the Blessing of God," &. O! the irresistible Charm of the Word *Such*!

Just as Erasmus has written a treatise in praise of folly, so Swift has Wharton promise to write "an Encomium upon

SUCH." "But whatever Changes our Language may undergo (and every thing that is *English* is given to change) this happy Word is sure to live in your immortal Preface."

Wharton is then made to quote a soaring passage from the Preface which contains the parenthesis "(and Oh that it had spared the Places Sacred to his Worship)", the *it* referring to "the Spirit of Discord." Swift makes Wharton comment:

Oh Exquisite! How pathetically does your Lordship complain of the Downfal of Whiggism, and *Daniel Burges's* Meeting-house! The generous Compassion your Lordship has shewn upon this tragical Occasion, makes me believe your Lordship would not be unaffected with an Accident that had like to have befallen a poor Whore of my Acquaintance about that Time, who being big with Whig, was so alarmed at the Rising of the Mob, that she had like to have miscarried upon it; for the Logical Jade presently concluded, (and the Inference was natural enough) that if they began pulling down Meeting-houses, it might end in demolishing those Houses of Pleasure, where she constantly paid her Devotion; and, indeed, there seems a close Connection between *Extempore* Prayer and *Extempore* Love. I doubt not, if this Disaster had reach'd your Lordship before, you would have found some Room in that moving *Parenthesis*, to have express'd your Concern for it.

I come now to that last Stroke of your Lordship's almighty Pen; I mean that expressive Dash—which you give when you come to the New Ministry, where you break off with an artful *Aposiopesis*, and by refusing to say any Thing of them yourself, leave your Readers to think the worst they possibly can. Here your Lordship shews yourself a most consummate Orator, when even your very Silence is thus eloquent.

Such criticism, cast as it is in specific rhetorical terminology, offers yet another instance of Swift's intimate knowledge of the art of rhetoric as a discipline.

One can easily see that rhetoric was not something that Swift merely employed, remaining silent on the art itself, but that, as can be observed over a wide span of his writing—from *A Tale of a Tub* to the sermons—rhetoric was a subject which Swift was constantly interested in and acutely aware of.

Swift's distinction between the elaborate rhetoric of a political pamphlet and the subdued rhetoric of a sermon is reflected in one of his letters to Stella. He tells her of his great fun in perpetrating the hoax of his account of Prior's negotiations in France to arrange for a separate peace with France. Referring to "A New Journey to Paris; Together with Some Secret Transactions between the French King and an English Gentleman. By The Sieur du Baudrier (Translated from the French)," he tells Stella it is "a grave formal lie." For exposition aimed at man's reason Swift used "plain honest stuff"; for his great ironies and much of his nonironical political writing Swift employed rhetoric to operate within any "grave formal lie" that suited his purpose.

## CHAPTER II

# "A Modest Proposal"

SWIFT'S best and most popular ironical essay, "A Modest Proposal," reveals Swift at once as master ironist and master classical rhetorician. In investigating the various elements of classical rhetoric employed in this essay and indicating how each functions either within the irony or to build the irony, I will explore the following major topics: the classical form of the essay; the ethical proof; the use of the two major rhetorical devices, diminution and refining; and the less frequently used devices.

## THE CLASSICAL FORM

The essay is organized in the manner of a classical oration, as follows:

| | | | | |
|---|---|---|---|---|
| Exordium | ---- | Paragraphs | 1 | through | 7 |
| Narration | ---- | Paragraphs | 8 | through | 16 |
| Digression | ---- | Paragraphs | 17 | through | 19 |
| Proof | ---- | Paragraphs | 20 | through | 28 |
| Refutation | ---- | Paragraphs | 29 | through | 30 |
| Peroration | ---- | Paragraphs | 31 | through | 33 |

The exordium includes three kinds of material, all of which are acceptable in a classical exordium: a pitiful description of the state of Ireland, intended to appeal to the emotions of the reader; statements which reflect the benevolence of the author, designed to establish the ethical proof; and hints and preparatory statements for the proof to follow.

The narration contains the statement of the proposal, with some further preparation for the proof.

Instead of going immediately into the proof, the projector inserts, in good classical form, a digression. Its subject matter parallels the subject matter of the essay by relating the custom of the Formosan court in eating the flesh of young girls whose bodies have just been cut down by the public hangman.

Following this digression containing the historical parallel is the proof, which contains six major reasons why the proposal should be accepted, plus the several summarized reasons.

In the refutation the projector brushes aside the single objection which he feels can reasonably be urged against him, that the population would be greatly decreased. He incorporates this argument into his own, claiming that it was one of his chief motives. He also sweeps aside the vain, visionary, and foolish "expedients" which have been offered in the past.

The peroration is made up of further statements which reflect favourably on the character of the projector and of a reiteration of the major topics of the essay. The appeal to the emotions stops one paragraph short of the end of the peroration. Just as Swift regularly undercuts a sentence with a fine irony at the end of the sentence, so he concludes the whole essay with a subdued minor point which is almost an ironic aside: in this case, his personal reference to the fact that his wife is past child-bearing.

The classical form of the essay is itself an important constituent of Swift's irony, for the projector's addressing his readers through an ancient and learned form helps to allay any suspicion of radical newness. A revolutionary new proposal is insinuated in a traditional, respected form.

## The Ethical Proof

The moral and ethical character of the pleader is one of the three major proofs designated by Aristotle.[1] This kind of proof is one of the main kinds employed by Swift in most of his satires and much of his other writing (especially in his role as Examiner). In varying degrees, every essay by him which has an "author" makes use of this kind of classical proof. The sources of this proof in any oration are two: the implicit indications of the moral character of the pleader and the explicit ones. The implicit ones are made up of the whole tone of the essay and are not to be isolated. The explicit ones are the overt indications throughout the speech. Swift has made use of his exordium to begin the explicit characterization by showing the projector's concern, compassion, and high motive in modestly suggesting this beneficial solution to the state of Ireland. This establishing the character and motives of the pleader is a standard use of the classical exordium.

The specific details by which Swift builds up the ethical proof fall into four categories descriptive of the projector: his humanity, his self-confidence, his competence in the immediate subject of the proposal, and his reasonableness.

The humanity of the projector is immediately revealed in the opening words of the address. While the projector is moving his audience to pity with his description of the "melancholy Object of those, who walk through the streets of this great Town," he is also indicating the humane inclinations of the speaker, who is also capable of being moved to such pity.

In the proof the projector reflects his compassion for the "poorer Tenants" who "will have something valuable of their own" if the proposal is put into effect. Later in the same section (paragraph 26) he cites as a reason for his proposal the kind and humane treatment it would assure expectant mothers, as well as its tendency to increase "the Care and Tenderness of Mothers toward their Children."

In the digression (paragraph 17) the projector objects to the proffered "Refinement" on his proposal (that young lads and maidens be used in place of venison) because "some scrupulous People might be apt to censure such a Practice (although indeed very unjustly) as a little bordering upon Cruelty; which, I confess, hath always been with me the strongest Objection against any Project, how well soever intended." In the litotes "a little bordering upon Cruelty" the projector accomplishes several purposes. He indicates his own humaneness in rejecting this refinement partially on grounds of cruelty. He gains an argumentative point by branding all other proposals as cruel also. Notice that he does not explicitly exclude his own proposal when he says, "which, I confess hath always been with me the strongest Objection against *any* Project." (Italics mine.) However, he recoups this hint of concession by observing that such an objection stems from too nice a scrupulosity.

In the last paragraph he assures the reader of his great sincerity and unselfish motives: "I PROFESS, in the Sincerity of my Heart, that I have not the least personal Interest, in endeavouring to promote this necessary Work. . . .I have no Children, by which I can propose to get a single Penny; the youngest being nine Years old, and my Wife past Childbearing." This last sentence gives two more pieces of information which are important to the character of the pleader. He is not a childless man who can propose such a solution in ignorance of a father's feelings, and he will not gain personally from the adoption of the proposal.

Because the projector of this proposal is sometimes thought of as the *ingénu* type, a somewhat diffident, inexperienced person who has come upon the scene without being in complete touch with the whole situation, it has not been sufficiently noticed that he is at the same time a bit cocksure.[2] In creating his projector, Swift faced a rhetorical problem that required the careful balancing of these rather contrasting characteristics in one person. He had to make the projector humble enough to gain the reader's approval and sympathy and confident enough to gain the reader's confidence in his ability and qualifications with the subject.[3] Added to this double problem is the fact that, while both of these ends were being accomplished, the projector had to be kept sufficiently dense to sustain the irony.

The self-confidence of the projector is first indicated in the second paragraph, in which, a bit presumptuously, he looks forward to seeing himself commemorated with a statue for being "a Preserver of the Nation." His sureness of himself and of the efficacy of his proposal is stated in a qualified form in the opening sentence of the narration: "I SHALL NOW therefore humbly propose my own Thoughts; which I hope will not be liable to the least Objection." and is echoed in the first sentence of the refutation: "I CAN think of no one Objection, that will possibly be raised against this Proposal; unless it should be urged, that the Number of People will be thereby much lessened in the Kingdom." This last, concessive clause is quickly done away with by the author's turning this single objection into an advantage for his cause.[4]

A pleader in the act of refuting naturally shows self-confidence. So does the projector when he tells us of his friend's suggesting that the lack of venison could be supplied by the youth of Ireland.

In paragraph nineteen the projector stands in contrast to "SOME Persons of desponding Spirit" who are in as great a concern for the aged as he is for the youth. He asserts that he is "not in the least Pain upon that matter": one could not reasonably expect the aged to be taken care of any more rapidly than they are by death, famine, and the like.

The projector speaks out boldly in introducing his proof: "I think the Advantages by the Proposal which I have made are obvious, and many, as well as of the highest Importance." And he proceeds to list and describe six of these advantages, but finally (implying that there are too many advantages to list) he summarizes the rest. Argument from a wealth of reasons indicates the firmness of the projector's position, since he can afford to waste them.

Closely related to the self-confidence of the pleader is his competence in dealing with the subject at hand. The projector gives abundant evidence that he is capable of dealing with the problem. First, he has not burst into print without first giving much thought and research to this problem: "As to my own Part, having turned my Thoughts for many Years, upon this important Subject, and maturely weighed the several *Schemes of other Projectors,* I have always found them grosly mistaken in their Computation." He then plunges into a barrage of mathematical calculations, which of course indicate his painstaking work and thought on the subject. In paragraph six he begins with the figure of 200,000 couples, from which he subtracts 30,000 who can maintain their own children. He subtracts 50,000 more couples whose children will not live. This leaves 120,000 couples to be provided for. In the next two sentences he states

I again subtract Fifty Thousand, for those Women who miscarry, or whose Children die by Accident, or Disease, within the Year. There only remain an Hundred and Twenty Thousand Children of poor Parents, annually born. . . .

The projector returns to the idea in paragraph ten: "the Hundred and Twenty Thousand Children, already computed. . . ." He subtracts 20,000 more children who are to be preserved for breeding, only one-fourth of these to be males.[5] It is this solid core of mathematics which makes the proposal so real and so practical—such a "fair, cheap, and easy Method."

This competence in calculations is reinforced by the vocabulary of the essay: "I HAVE reckoned upon a Medium. . . ." "As to our City of *Dublin*; Shambles may be appointed for this Purpose. . . ." "SUPPOSING that one Thousand Families in this City, . . . I compute. . . ."

In addition to such verbal indicants of competence, the whole movement of the proof reflects the strong debater arguing from a wealth of material. Six carefully thought out advantages are brought forward in such a way as to imply that he could continue listing advantages indefinitely, but finally he stops, being (as he says) "studious of Brevity." His two large rhetorical questions in paragraph thirty-two which he poses to his would-be answerers complement this listing by indicating movingly and thoroughly the consequence which will obtain if the proposal is not accepted. Thus, both through the careful attention to the smallest detail and through the marshalling of the whole movement of the essay, Swift has succeeded in creating an aura of rightness in the carefully thought out and convincingly presented proposal.

The reasonableness of the pleader, the fourth heading under which the character of the projector is established, is amply provided for by Swift. A reference already cited in another connection is also to the point here: "as to my own Part, having turned my Thoughts for many years, upon this important Subject. . . ." This careful deliberation suggests a reasonable rather than a rash pleader. "AFTER all, I am not so violently bent upon my own Opinion, as to reject any Offer proposed by wise Men, which shall be found equally cheap, easy, and effectual."

The projector reflects his reasonableness by the conservative nature of his calculations. In establishing 30,000 as the number of couples who can maintain their own children, he says, "although I apprehend there cannot be so many, *under the present Distresses of the Kingdom*. . . ."

Concession occurs again in the same paragraph.[6] The projector states that children under six are seldom good thieves, "although, I must confess, they learn the Rudiments [of stealing] much earlier."

In allowing that of the 20,000 reserved for breeders, only one-fourth will be males, the projector through concession emphasizes the generosity of his calculation, for this proportion "is more than we allow to *Sheep, black Cattle,* or *Swine.*" The projector, in declining the "worthy Person's" refinement on his scheme (that the bodies of young lads and maidens between the ages of twelve and fourteen could be used for venison), concedes that here would be a slight chance for cruelty, "which, I confess, hath always been with me the strongest Objection against any Project, how well soever intended."

In describing the Formosan practice of court ministers' buying the bodies of young girls fresh from the gibbet, the projector concedes, "Neither indeed can I deny, that if the same Use were made of several plump young girls of this Town" the kingdom might be better off.

Most of these concessions are of little importance to the projector's central argument, but their use, where they cannot damage the proposition, tends to create an impression in the reader of the projector's reasonableness and lack of dogmatism.

Closely associated with this device of concession is that of deference to superiors (a device greatly needed in the Roman courts of the Empire, especially when an important or powerful personage had to be attacked but attacked politely). The projector graciously defers to the "worthy Person" who had offered a refinement on his scheme. "But with due Deference to so excellent a Friend, and so deserving a Patriot, I cannot be altogether in his Sentiments." Such use of the young girls would be wasteful because they soon would become producers of this new food: "Then, as to the Females, it would, I think, with humble Submission, *be a Loss to the Public,* because they soon would become Breeders themselves. . . ."

Actually, of course, the projector concedes nothing; neither does he really defer to anyone. However, a tone of concession and of deference is present and contributes to the ethical proof.

I have said that the projector is a bit cocksure. He is also manifestly humble and modest. The proposal is a "modest" one. It is introduced in generally modest terms: "I SHALL NOW therefore humbly propose my own Thoughts . . ."; "I do humbly offer to *publick Consideration.* . . ." Swift has blended these two qualities of his projector in such a way that both are convincing and that neither quality overshadows the other. The result is a pleader whose humility is justifiably tempered by the sure knowledge that he has something to offer Ireland, to her everlasting benefit.

These are the explicit indicants of the moral character of the pleader; they are reinforced and dramatized by the whole tone of the essay. From this stable personality Swift allows only one outburst of real anger and pathos. It occurs at the climax of the essay, when the patient but exhausted old projector, "having been wearied out for many Years with offering vain, idle, visionary Thoughts," turns in righteous indignation to insist: "THEREFORE I repeat, let no Man talk to me of these and the like Expedients; till he hath, at least, a Glimpse of Hope, that there will ever be some hearty and sincere Attempt to put *them in Practice.*"

### Diminution

The principle of diminution is the informing device of the entire essay; it underlies the whole animal motif. This diminution of man to animal Quintana sees in its perfected form in Book IV of *Gulliver's Travels* and in "A Modest Proposal." It is, he says, perhaps "the most devastating weapon ever used by a satirist."[7]

Swift's use of the device of diminution will be found to take three general directions, the first being the most pervasive: the creation of the illusion of animality, the substitution of the lesser word, and the imputation of the lesser motive.

The most obvious form of diminution is the use of the lesser noun to refer to people—especially to mothers and fathers. Strolling mothers are *"Beggars* of the female Sex." As if speaking of any mammal, the projector comments that "It is true a Child, *just dropped from its Dam,* may be supported by her Milk for a solar Year with little other Nourishment. . . ." In the mathematical working out of how many

babies to save, the projector refers to the couples merely as
"Breeders."[8] Only a fourth part of these "breeders" are to be
male "which is more than we allow to *Sheep, black Cattle,
or Swine. . . .*" Like other animals, the mother will be able to
work "until she produceth another Child."

As there are certain seasons when most animals foal, the
projector with the help of a grave author finds that the human
animals will produce most in December and January. He
reckons that the markets will be most glutted a year after Lent.[9]

There will be no lack of people willing to set up butchery
shambles in Dublin; however, "I rather recommend buying
the Children alive, and dressing them hot from the Knife, as
we do *roasting Pigs.*" The *"true Lover of his Country"* has
suggested that, "many fine Gentlemen of this Kingdom, having
of late destroyed their Deer," "the Want of Venison might
well be supplied by the Bodies of young Lads and Maidens,
not exceeding fourteen Years of Age or under Twelve."

As if referring to cattle, the projector calculates that since
the cost of maintaining 100,000 children after the age of two
can be estimated at not less than ten shillings *per annum*, "the
nation's Stock will be thereby increased Fifty Thousand
Pounds *per annum*. . . ." (There is here a pun upon stock
as livestock, as financial stock, and as pantry stock.)

"Men would become as *fond* of their Wives, during the
time of their Pregnancy, as they are now of their *Mares* in
Foal, their *Cows* in *Calf*, or *Sows* when they are ready to
farrow. . . ." Beyond the equating the expectant mothers
to animals, there is here the implication that men are humane
to their animals and not to their wives.

Not only will a "well-grown fat yearling Child" well
grace a Lord Mayor's feast, but also the projector can depend
upon the pride of the women as to *"which of them could
bring the fattest Child to the Market."* The "Customers of
Infants Flesh" would in Dublin alone "take off, annually,
about Twenty Thousand Carcasses; and the rest of the Kingdom (where probably they will be sold somewhat cheaper)
the remaining Eighty Thousand."

At the beginning of the mathematical calculations the
people were referred to as "souls," but at the end they have
become "Creatures in human Figure," "Mouths and Backs."

It is easy to get the impression from reading the essay casually that Swift creates the animal transfer by avoiding the use of terms appropriate to human beings. But this is not quite true. *Mother, father, child, children, babe, youth, lad, maiden, infant* are liberally sprinkled throughout the essay. With the exception of the word *carcass* (used in reference to children in paragraphs 15, 27, and 28) all of the other nouns applied to children are terms for food (see the next paragraph, below). In addition to the use of a lower term, Swift effects the animal diminution by juxtaposition of modifier and noun, as in "yearling Child." Rhetorically, the projector's constantly varying the normal term with the animal term serves to keep the reader off guard, with the result that if the reader begins to expect the animal term, he is fooled. The resulting effect is that one term is just as normal as the other. The animal terms are slipped in unobtrusively, and they are never insisted upon.

As if the diminution of human beings to animals were not strong enough, the irony is intensified by a species of redoubled diminution: the animal becomes food. The progression of diminution thus becomes man to animal to food (with the obvious implication that man is an animal to eat such food, or even worse than an animal, there being relatively few animals which are cannibalistic). Notice the final step in the diminution to food in the following statements. A "young healthy Child, well nursed, is, at a Year old, a most delicious, nourishing, and wholesome Food; whether *stewed, roasted, baked* or *boiled*; and I make no doubt, that it will equally serve in a *Fricasie*, or *Ragoust*." They will be "plump and fat for a good Table. A Child will make two Dishes at an Entertainment for Friends; and when the family dines alone, the fore or hind Quarter will make a reasonable Dish; and seasoned with a little Pepper or Salt, will be very good Boiled on the fourth Day, especially in *Winter*." One of Swift's most devastating techniques of word order is the final twist or insinuation with which he can charge the last phrase of a sentence. Witness the last phrase of the preceding sentence.

This new food will be "somewhat dear" and therefore "very *proper for Landlords*; who, as they have already *devoured* [italics mine] most of the Parents, seem to have the best Title to the Children."

If such man-to-animal diminution stood alone in the essay, it would no doubt be so offensive that it would defeat its intended purpose of persuading the reader. However, as Swift has blended the operation of this device with the functioning of the several other devices, the whole resultant fabric of the irony is made so tight-knit that this particular use of diminution is one highly successful and basic to the whole essay. The steady reiteration of this diminution tends to establish it in the reader's consciousness as a norm, and thus the rhetorical device becomes one of the means of establishing the ironic norm of the essay. Obviously care had to be exercised not to overplay the device lest it boomerang. Swift so manipulates its use that by slipping in a word here and a phrase there, the impression of normalness (and the resultant acceptance) is gradually achieved.

All of the uses of diminution in this essay are not concerned directly with the animal figure, although, since the other uses of the device contribute to the dehumanizing tone of the whole essay, they can be said to contribute indirectly. The remaining uses are of two kinds: the use of the worse word to name a thing and the assumption of the worse motive in the performance of an act.

In paragraph two the "Children" in Ireland become "a very great additional Grievance." And in paragraph nineteen the old people are "a grievous. . . . Incumbrance." A mother can nourish her child for a solar year on as little as two shillings, "which the Mother may certainly get, or the Value in Scraps, by her lawful Occupation of *Begging*."

The proposal will prevent "those *voluntary Abortions*, and that horrid Practice of *Women murdering their Bastard Children*; alas! too frequent among us; sacrificing the *poor innocent Babes*, I doubt, more to avoid the Expence than the Shame; which would move Tears and Pity in the most Savage and inhuman Breast." There are two kinds of diminution in this sentence. The lesser motive is imputed when the projector states that the mothers will so act in order to avoid the expense rather than the shame, and animality is implied when the projector observes that such an act would move a savage or an inhuman breast to tears. The few casual references to savages, Laplanders, and the inhabitants of Topinamboo combine to suggest to the reader that here are some people who might well be emulated. These references also provide a further standard by which the ironic norm can through contrast be brought into even sharper focus.

Swift's extensive use of diminution can be studied advantageously in tabular form. The following table presents a graphic summary of all of the nouns and a few of the verbs and modifiers which Swift has used in the diminution from man to animal, indicating the extent, the incidence, and the gradations of diminution.

## PARENTS

| Paragraph Number | Best Name | Impersonal or Less Name | Animal or Food Term |
|---|---|---|---|
| 1 | mothers | female sex | |
| 2 | mothers fathers | beggars | |
| 3 | parents | | |
| 4 | parents | | dam |
| 5 | | women | |
| 6 | wives | souls women | breeders |
| | poor parents parents | | |
| 10 | mother | | |
| 12 | parents | | |
| 14 | mother | beggars cottagers labourers farmers tenants | produceth another child |
| 17 | parents | nearest relations | breeders |
| 19 | | females aged, diseased, mained poor people young labourers | |

| 21 |         | papists          | breeders          |
|----|---------|------------------|-------------------|
|    |         | dangerous enemies |                  |
|    |         | good protestants  |                  |
| 22 |         | poor tenants      |                  |
| 24 |         |                   | constant breeders |
| 26 | mothers | men               |                  |
|    | wives   | married women     |                  |
| 29 |         | women             |                  |
|    |         | shop-keepers      |                  |
| 32 | parents | beggars           | breed            |
|    | wives   | beggars           |                  |
|    |         | cottagers         |                  |
|    |         | labourers         |                  |
| 33 |         | the poor          |                  |

## CHILDREN

| Paragraph Number | Best Name | Impersonal or Less Name | Animal or Food Term |
|------------------|-----------|-------------------------|---------------------|
| 1  | children  |                  |                        |
|    | helpless  |                  |                        |
|    | infants   |                  |                        |
| 2  | children  | grievance        |                        |
|    | children  |                  |                        |
| 3  | children  |                  |                        |
|    | infants   |                  |                        |
| 4  | child     |                  | just dropped from      |
| 5  | innocent  |                  | dam                    |
|    | babes     | bastard children |                        |
| 6  | children  |                  | number                 |
|    | children  |                  | probationary thieves   |
|    | children  |                  |                        |
| 7  | boy       |                  |                        |
|    | girl      |                  |                        |
| 9  | child     |                  | wholesome food         |
| 10 | children  | males            | for breed              |
|    | children  | male             | two dishes             |
|    | child     | females          |                        |
| 11 | child     |                  |                        |
| 12 | children  |                  |                        |

| Paragraph Number | Best Name | Impersonal or Less Name | Animal or Food Term |
|---|---|---|---|
| 13 | | Papist infants | infant's flesh |
| 14 | child | beggar's child | carcass of a good fat child |
| | | | 4 dishes of nutritive meat |
| 15 | | | carcass |
| 16 | children | | bought alive & dressed hot, as we do pigs |
| 17 | | bodies of lads and maidens | for venison |
| | | | flesh |
| | | both sexes | |
| | | males | |
| 18 | | young person | carcass a prime dainty |
| | | body of plump girl | |
| | | plump young girls | |
| 23 | children | | new dish |
| | | | goods |
| 24 | children | | |
| 25 | | | food |
| 26 | children | | fattest child at the market |
| | babes | | |
| 27 | | | carcasses |
| | | | fat well-grown yearling child |
| 28 | | | infant's flesh |
| 29 | | | carcasses |
| 31 | | | commodity |
| | | | flesh |
| 32 | children | mouths | |
| | | backs | |
| | | mortals | |
| 33 | infants | | |
| | children | | |

Swift refers to the parents by the best name sixteen times, by the impersonal name twenty-eight times, and by the animal name eight times. Naming them most frequently by the im-

personal middle term is consistent with his purpose of neu-
tralizing these human beings so that, on the eight occasions
of referring to them in animal terms, easy acceptance of the
animal terms results. By firmly establishing the middle term,
Swift has not had to make the broad jump from human being
to animal; he moves only from the middle or neutral term to
the animal term.

The acceptance of the parents as breeders of animals makes
the acceptance of babies as animals much easier. Thus, by
natural sequence, the parent-as-animal diminution serves as
preparation for the babies-as-animals diminution. It further
allows for the larger number of references to the children as
animals and as food. Swift refers to the children by the best
name twenty-nine times, by the impersonal name sixteen
times, and by the animal name twenty-four times. The low
incidence of the middle term in naming children results from
the foundation laid by its high incidence in naming parents.
(This balance results not from a chronological sequence in the
essay but from the sequence in nature, that the offspring will
naturally be like the parents.) Building the diminution carefully in this manner, Swift was free then to push the terrible
juxtaposition of the two extremes, the best name coupled with
the animal or food name for children.

It is through observing and understanding each such careful handling by Swift of a particular device of rhetoric that
one comes better to comprehend the full implications of Swift's
rhetorical art and its contribution to his irony. Only thus can
we begin to explain most readers' amazement reflected in the
question, "How does he get away with rendering human
beings as animals in a few brief paragraphs?" His painstaking
manipulation of rhetoric supplies the answer.

## REFINING

Refining "consists in dwelling on the same topic and yet
seeming to say something new."[10] It can be accomplished by
a variation in words, in delivery, or in treatment (e.g., by a
change in the form—to dialogue, to characterization, etc.).
The device appears in Swift's essay; however, it is put to a
much subtler use than the author of *Ad Herennium* had in
mind. Swift's use of refining is akin to what Martin Price has

called "redefinition":[11] in referring to something, Swift varies
the word until finally the word or phrase has a new meaning,
a meaning which Swift intended it to have all along but which
he carefully avoided expressing.

For example, the proposal is ostensibly designed for the
children of professional beggars, who hardly make up a
majority of the population. Swift must redefine "professional
Beggar" so as to include all of the poor within this term. The
pride of the poor is as great as the pride of the rich; therefore
Swift eases the redefinition in by "refining" it, by varying
the terms without seeming to dwell on them. This is accomplished in three steps and reinforced in a fourth (paragraphs
2, 3, 14, and 32, in that order). The pitiful strollers in paragraph one are said to be beggars (whether technically professional beggars is not made clear). In paragraph three the
projector states, "BUT my Intention is very far from being
confined to provide only for the Children of *professed Beggars*: It is of a much greater Extent, and shall take in the
whole Number of Infants at a certain Age, who are born
of Parents, in effect as little able to support them, as those
who demand our Charity in the Streets." The two groups
(the beggars and the poor) are put on one footing, but they
remain two groups. In the next several paragraphs all of the
mathematical calculations are concerned with "the Children
of the Poor," beggars not being mentioned. Swift waits until
paragraph fourteen to push the identification: "I HAVE already computed the Charge of nursing a Beggar's Child (in
which List I reckon all *Cottagers, Labourers,* and Four fifths of
the *Farmers*). . . ." The identification is complete, and it has
been accomplished by a quite casual parenthesis. The word
*beggar* is used only once again in the essay: in the peroration,
where the projector states "adding those who are Beggars by
profession, to the Bulk of Farmers, Cottagers, and Labourers,
with their Wives and Children, who are Beggars in Effect."
Through such refining Swift has steered a precarious course:
he has made the identification of the poor and the beggars and
at the same time he has refined so subtly that he has not im-
pugned the dignity of the group in whose behalf he is writing.

But all of Swift's refining is not so gentle; neither is it
aimed at redefinition. The landlords fare far worse. The word

*landlord* (or its equivalent "Gentleman of Fortune") occurs eleven times. The refining is merely verbal, and these words occur with iterative force to drive home the idea that the landlords will be the main eaters of this new food. This accusation against the landlords is prepared for in paragraphs six through ten, in which this new food is discussed. Who will eat it is only implied, until finally, late in paragraph ten, the projector states that these babies are to be "offered in Sale to *Persons of Quality* and *Fortune* through the Kingdom. . . ." The verb *offered* does not yet explicitly mean that these persons will accept the offer. Then in paragraph twelve the projector concedes that the food "will be somewhat dear, and therefore very *proper for Landlords*; who, as they have already devoured most of the Parents, seem to have the best Title to the Children." From this bold statement forward, the idea is not allowed to rest. In paragraph fourteen, it is repeated twice: "no Gentleman would repine to give Ten Shillings for the *Carcase of a good fat Child.* . . . thus the Squire will learn to be a good Landlord, and grow popular with his Tenants. . . ." In the next paragraph (15) we are told that the flayed carcasses will "make admirable *Gloves for Ladies,* and *Summer Boots for fine Gentlemen.*"

In the very next paragraph (16) the idea is implied in the discussion of the butchering of new food. And in the paragraph following (17), we meet the "VERY worthy person, *a true Lover of his Country,*" "so excellent a Friend, and so deserving a Patriot" who sees a way to refine this modest proposal. This is followed in the next paragraph by the story of the usage of the Formosan court (with the parallel implied).

The refining continues in paragraph twenty-two: "SECONDLY, the poorer Tenants will have something valuable of their very own, which, by Law, may be made liable to Distress, and help to pay their Landlord's Rent; their Corn and Cattle being already seized, and *Money a Thing Unknown.*"

The third reason given in favor of the proposal is that a new dish will be introduced to the tables of "all *Gentlemen of Fortune* in the Kingdom, who have any Refinement of Taste. . . ." The fifth reason is that the trade of "Houses frequented by all the *fine Gentlemen,* who justly value themselves upon their Knowledge in good Eating" will be greatly

increased, especially in houses where there is a "skilful Cook,
who understands how to oblige his Guests" and who "will
contrive to make it as expensive as they please."

Omitting it in the next paragraph, Swift returns to the
idea in the following one (27), as he visualizes the new food
at all fine tables, at the Lord Mayor's feast, and (in paragraph
28) at all "*merry Meetings*" such as "*Weddings and Christen-
ings.*" (It is appropriate to the subject matter that he should
single out these two occasions as examples of merry meetings.)

In the next paragraph (29) come the "Expedients" which
the projector rejects. The landlords are implied in several of
them, and near the end of the series are singled out: "*Of
teaching Landlords to have, at least, one Degree of Mercy towards their Tenants.*" In the peroration the landlords are hit
two more times. They are blamed for much of the "perpetual
Scene of Misfortunes," since tenants are borne down upon
by "the *Oppression of Landlords. . . .*" And in the final paragraph in the recapitulation the landlords are given the strong
final position in that series: "*and giving some pleasure to the
Rich.*"

Isolating all of these examples tends to give the impression
that Swift's amazingly frequent repetition of this idea is not
"refining" but merely gross pounding at a theme. However,
as each instance appears in full context, Swift's subtlety is fully
appreciated. Swift's refining is a rhetorical device contributing
to the reader's acceptance of the irony, because its operation
is pervasive, it works by indirection and by implication, it is
manipulated through a careful handling of the language of each
sentence, and because, when it appears, the reader's attention
is frequently fixed elsewhere (on the idea of the sentence
rather than on the method of the sentence).

## LESS FREQUENTLY USED DEVICES

Among less frequently used, but no less important, rhetorical devices of the "Modest Proposal" is appeal to authority.
In the exordium the projector assumes that all agree as to the
state of the kingdom: "I THINK that it is agreed by all
Parties, that this prodigious Number of Children in the Arms,
or on the Backs, or at the *Heels* of their *Mothers,* and frequently their *Fathers,* is *in the present deplorable State of the*

*Kingdom,* a very great additional Grievance. . . ." This appeal is of particular importance to Swift's English readers, for (as indicated in his "A Short View of the State of Ireland") many Englishmen, who were well entertained in fine houses during brief visits to Ireland, actually thought that Ireland was a prosperous kingdom and reported so back home.

"A principal Gentleman in the County of *Cavan*" has informed the projector that even in that county, which is famous for its thieves, there were not known to that gentleman over one or two instances in which children under the age of six were very skillful at stealing.

The projector has consulted the merchants, men who really should know about market prices, etc., in order to confirm his calculations, and he has been "assured by our Merchants" that children around the age of twelve are "no saleable Commodity."

Probably the most impressive single authority which the projector calls upon is that "grave" French author and physician, Rabelais, who has proved that a fish diet greatly contributes to potency in engendering this new commodity.

In addition to these explicit appeals to authority there are several implicit appeals. Each time that the projector says that certain gentlemen would pay this or that for various parts of this animal, or that such and such can be done to this commodity to please the gentlemen of fashion, he is presupposing the approval of these gentlemen. In fact one such gentleman—"a VERY worthy person, *a true Lover of his Country*" becomes so enthusiastic about the projector's plan that he "was pleased . . . to offer a Refinement on my Scheme." The older youths could be used as a substitute for venison. But the moderation of Swift's projector finds this suggestion excessive. Besides, "a very knowing American" has assured the projector that such meat is tough.

The implicit approval of authority is reflected in the following remarks which are scattered at random through the essay. "No Gentleman would repine to give Ten Shillings for the *Carcase of a good fat Child.*" The flayed carcass would make admirable gloves and summer boots. The landlords will have excellent nutritive meat "when he hath some particular Friend, or his own Family, to dine with him." Such meat would make a "considerable Figure" at a Lord Mayor's feast. These and the several other food passages in the essay completely presuppose participation in and approval of the scheme by the people of quality.

The explicit appeals to authority, especially to experts and grave authors, are standard in classical rhetoric. The indirect and implied approvals just enumerated, however, contribute more to the ironic trap than do the explicit ones, for the former imply a general acceptation among society. Appeal to the authority of the whole society is what Aristotle calls the appeal to "previous judgment," to a "necessary truth." If the truth is not necessary, then it can be an appeal to "the opinion held by the majority, or the wise, or all or most of the good."[12]

The device of interrogation is employed once in the essay. It is in the powerful thirty-second paragraph. This paragraph opens with the quite mild concession that the projector is "not so violently bent" upon his own opinion that he will not entertain other proposals. He merely makes one reservation: that any such projectors answer two questions:

*First*, As Things now stand, how they will find Food and Raiment, for a Hundred Thousand useless Mouths and Backs? And *secondly*, There being a round Million of Creatures in human Figure, throughout this Kingdom; whose whole Subsistence, put into a common Stock, would leave them in Debt two Millions of Pounds *Sterling*; adding those, who are Beggars by Profession, to the Bulk of Farmers, Cottagers, and Labourers, with their Wives and Children, who are Beggars in Effect; I desire those Politicians, who dislike my Overture, and may perhaps be so bold to attempt an Answer, that they first ask the Parents of these Mortals, Whether they would not, at this Day, think it a great Happiness to have been sold for Food at a Year old, in the Manner I prescribe; and thereby have avoided such a perpetual Scene of Misfortunes, as they have gone through; by the *Oppression of Landlords*; the Impossibility of paying Rent, without Money or Trade; the Want of common Sustenance, with neither House nor Cloaths, to cover them from the Inclemencies of Weather; and the most inevitable Prospect of entailing the like, or greater Miseries upon their Breed forever.

The final phrase "upon their Breed forever" has the inverted

ring of the finality of a prayer "world without end, amen."
This rhetorical question serves several purposes. It summarizes
the complaints which have been scattered throughout the
essay (the quotation is from the peroration); it is so couched
that what has been given in mass would have to be refuted
separately (a device which Quintilian recommends when a
pleader has massed together what cannot be strong separately);
and of course it gives the projector occasion to voice his most
stinging indictment without seeming to propound, since he
is merely posing a question as the basis for a possible concession
on his part.

Argument by elimination is scarcely used in this essay,
and in the passages in which it appears it does not occur
in its full syllogistic form. It is a telling means of persuasion because it narrows the argument by excluding any consideration except the one being urged.

The passage just quoted from paragraph thirty-two is a
good example of elimination, for if either question can reasonably be answered, the projector has already promised that
he is ready to concede and entertain other proposals. And
in paragraph nineteen in reference to the problem of old
people, the projector eliminates all other problems except
the one of his proposal, thus sharpening the focus on his
own proposal and making the audience more ready to attack
this problem with this solution, since this proposal will relieve
the whole economic situation and all members of the society.

Swift uses the device of accumulation to good effect in
two instances, one of which has just been quoted from paragraph thirty-two. The second question posed there is a long
series which accurately and adequately summarizes the whole
situation of Ireland and the modest proposal being made.

The other use of accumulation is the brief description in
the final paragraph: "having no other motive than the *Publick
Good of my Country, by advancing our Trade, providing for
Infants, relieving the Poor, and giving some Pleasure to the
Rich.*" This series concisely echoes each of the major groups
of reasons which have been set forth (except the antipapist
reasons, which might, from the point of view of the projector,
be included "in the public Good"). It is natural that both
instances of accumulation in this essay should occur in the

peroration, for recapitulation is one of the standard uses of this section of the speech.

From the understatement of the essay's title forward, litotes has an unusually strong force, since it operates within the ironic inversion. Statements which would be quite ordinary understatement are surcharged by the ironically inverted context. In paragraph twelve the projector grants that this new "Food will be somewhat dear." In an essay which is *not* built upon irony of inversion, litotes operates merely to indicate more force by couching an idea in a less forceful manner than is appropriate. But to say that this food "will be somewhat dear" lifts the ironic veil in order to state a terrible truth. And the statement comes through in all its truth, with only the one word "somewhat" holding the thin thread of irony as the observation darts for the moment to the very edge of the fine line between irony and simple truth.

The same effect is achieved in paragraph seventeen. (The reference is to ,the gentleman's suggestion that young boys and girls could be used as a substitute for vension.):

And besides it is not improbable, that some scrupulous People might be apt to censure such a Practice (although indeed very unjustly) as a little bordering upon Cruelty; which, I confess, hath always been with me the strongest Objection against any Project, how well soever intended.

The single phrase "a little bordering on" holds the ironic structure tightly together during the moment that the ironist, brushing aside all except a single thin layer of irony, allows his reader a glimpse into the heart of the matter, which is that any mere proposal is cruelly fruitless since only a thoroughly normal and healthy administration of the kingdom can give genuine well-being to Ireland.

In the list of rejected "expedients" the litotes has the same function. Two of the expedients are expressed in litotes: "*Of being a little cautious not to sell our Country and Consciences for nothing: Of teaching Landlords to have, at least, one Degree of Mercy towards their Tenants.*" The litotes is strong just in these isolated examples. But, when they are set into ironic inversion, they gain added power: Let no man talk to me of being a little cautious not to sell our country and consciences for nothing; let no man talk to me of teaching landlords to have, at least, one degree of mercy toward their tenants. The negative of "Let no man talk to me" further emphasizes the already negative litotes of the *of* phrases.

Although the passage listing the expedients is not cast as a whole into litotes, the effect of the whole is quite similar to that which I have just described in connection with litotes: the ironist momentarily holds aside all but one of the several curtains of irony so that his reader may be shown the truth.

Therefore, let no man talk to me of other Expedients: Of taxing our Absentees at five Shillings a Pound; Of using neither Cloaths, nor Household Furniture except what is of our own Growth and Manufacture: Of utterly rejecting the Materials and Instruments that promote foreign Luxury: Of curing the Expensiveness of Pride, Vanity, Idleness, and Gaming in our Women: Of introducing a Vein of Parsimony, Prudence and Temperance: Of learning to love our Country, wherein we differ even from LAPLANDERS, and the Inhabitants of TOPINAMBOO: Of quitting our Animosities, and Factions; nor act any longer like the JEWS, who were murdering one another at the very Moment their City was taken: Of being a little cautious not to sell our Country and Consciences for nothing: Of teaching Landlords to have, at least, one Degree of Mercy towards their Tenants. Lastly, Of putting a Spirit of Honesty, Industry, and Skill into our Shopkeepers; who, if a Resolution could now be taken to buy only our native Goods, would immediately unite to cheat and exact upon us in the Price, the Measure, and the Goodness; nor could ever yet be brought to make one fair Proposal of just Dealing, though often and earnestly invited to it.

Swift has left no doubt as to his real meaning: this is the only extended passage in the essay which is italicized; it is the only extended passage built upon the principle of understatement. The use of litotes is heavily limited in this essay (occurring only in the passages which have just been discussed) because the rhetoric is geared to the irony: litotes is the device which allows the ironist the thinnest facade of pretense, and obviously Swift could not allow his ironic pose to become fragile at too many points.

The projector makes several appeals directly to the emotions of his audience. One such appeal is to his reader's prejudice against Roman Catholics. Three separate passages contain this appeal. In the first paragraph of the essay such an appeal is prepared for. The "helpless infants" of these starving parents will, when they grow up, become thieves, "or leave their *dear Native Country, to fight for the Pretender in* Spain, or sell themselves to the *Barbadoes*." The next passage is in paragraph thirteen. The projector has been assured that

. . . *Fish being a prolifick Dyet*, there are more Children born in *Roman Catholick Countries* about Nine Months after *Lent*, than at any other Season: Therefore reckoning a Year after *Lent*, the Markets will be more glutted than usual; because the Number of *Popish Infants*, is, at least, three to one in this Kingdom; and therefore it will have one other Collateral Advantage, by lessening the Number of *Papists* among us.

The subject is mentioned once more; it has the lead position in the reasons of the proof:

FOR, *First*, as I have already observed, it would greatly lessen the *Number of Papists*, with whom we are yearly over-run; being the principal Breeders of the Nation, as well as our most dangerous Enemies; and who stay at home on Purpose, with a Design to *deliver the Kingdom to the Pretender*; hoping to take their Advantage by the Absence of *so many good Protestants*, who have chosen rather to leave their Country, than stay at home, and pay Tithes against their Conscience, to an idolatrous *Episcopal Curate*.

Stigmatizing the Roman Catholics as traitors and scolding the Anglo-Irish for not staying home and for not supporting the Established Church play right to the opinion of the Anglo-Irish. Swift's making this particular appeal raises the old and unanswerable question of whether he directed his Irish tracts to the whole of Ireland or to the Anglo-Irish minority.[13] If it is to all Irishmen, this device is hardly a happy choice.

The projector, with a sure knowledge of his readers' prejudice, appeals to their prejudice against dishonest shopkeepers. His appeal has a position in the long, italicized catalogue of rejected "expedients":

Lastly, Of putting a Spirit of Honesty, Industry, and Skill into our Shop-keepers; who, if a Resolution could now be taken to buy only our native Goods, would immediately unite to cheat and exact upon us in the Price, the Measure, and the Goodness; nor could ever yet be brought to make one fair Proposal of just Dealing, though often and earnestly invited to it.

The statement comes with all the more force and conviction, for Swift had so often and earnestly invited them to it. This appeal works equally well to the general prejudice against shop-keepers or to the Anglo-Irish prejudice against Irish shop-keepers (in the event that the essay was directed mainly to the Anglo-Irish).

A favorite device of rhetorical appeal to the emotions is that of the "vivid picture" or, as it is sometimes called, "ocular demonstration."[14] Vividness being a standard quality in the best work of Swift, it might seem a bit beside the point to single out particular instances of this quality here. The rhetorical device is, however, usually meant to name an extended set piece of description. In addition to the general quality of vividness throughout Swift's essay, there is one of these set pieces: the opening paragraph. In this first paragraph of the exordium Swift sketches in minute detail the picture of the wandering, begging mothers and children. The device becomes even more obvious when we consider that in an essay to *prove* the validity of a proposal, the essay begins, not with a statement of the proposal, not with any preliminary arguments for the proposal, but with an actual picture of what has brought about the need for the proposal. In this sense the opening paragraph is an ocular demonstration. This is the only set picture in the essay; other passages which describe a situation tend to do so in terms too abstract or in a point of view too generalized and abstracted to give such a set picture. There are little phrases which, however, through the sure touch of the poet, give glances at little pictures, such as the final clause in this sentence: "We should soon see an honest Emulation among the married women, *which of them could bring the fattest Child to the Market.*" The last clause gives us a scene of proud and bragging mothers elbowing and vying with each other at the market place. However, such little touches tend to be more a matter of style than of rhetorical device.

Swift's use of parenthesis in the essay functions in four ways: two are used to introduce allusions which enrich the argument by suggesting situations never stated or explained; three are used to slip in cutting asides reflecting the judgment of the projector; one is used in connection with diminution; and another is used in balance with litotes.

The two which allude to arguments not specifically raised in the essay are the following: the projector points out that there is no opportunity for the employment of laborers in handicraft and agriculture: "We neither build Houses, (I mean in the Country) nor cultivate Land." The parenthesis clarifies the point. The projector does not mean primarily that construction jobs are lacking; he means that no great plantation houses are being built and that therefore there are no agricultural jobs being created. The other parenthesis of this kind is on the same subject: Dublin alone would "take off, annually, about Twenty Thousand Carcasses; and the rest of the Kingdom (where probably they will be sold somewhat cheaper) the remaining Eighty Thousand." The parenthesis again emphasizes the unfruitful conditions in the country areas. He has told his readers of the terrible conditions in Dublin, and through these two parentheses he leaves it to the reader to imagine the situation in the country, a situation even worse than that in Dublin.[15] The wealth of argument which the projector enjoys is so vast that only through these two parentheses does he have space even to indicate some lines of proof for his proposal. This is one of the most subtle refinements Swift has given to a standard rhetorical device.

In three instances Swift uses parenthesis in its more usual function of inserting an aside to his audience: "THOSE who are more thrifty (*as I must confess the Times require*) may flay the Carcase. . . ." He accomplishes little here with the parenthesis because his use of italics emphasizes what the parenthesis is supposed to tuck in unobtrusively.[16] In a similar instance, the same device has much more power because italics are used for only one word and because the remark is so cutting: this proposal will insure a more humane treatment of wives by husbands, who will no longer "offer to beat or kick them, (as is too *frequent* a Practice) for fear of a Miscarriage." "There is likewise another Advantage in my *Scheme*, that it will prevent those *voluntary Abortions*, and that horrid Practice of *Women murdering their Bastard Children;* alas! too frequent among us; sacrificing their *poor innocent Babes.* . . ."

Two occasions of Swift's use of parenthesis are crucial to the passages in which they occur. Both have been discussed above, in connection with litotes and diminution, respectively. As has been noticed above, the projector has been careful gradually to refine *beggar* so that it will include all of the poor of Ireland. At the delicate point where the identification is completely made, parenthesis is brought into play to perform this task: "I HAVE already computed the Charge of nursing a Beggar's Child (in which list I reckon all *Cottagers, Labourers*, and Four fifths of the *Farmers*). . . ."

As we have seen, too, the passages in the essay where Swift employs litotes become thin in respect to the degree of irony present. In one such instance Swift uses parenthesis to help balance the litotes: some people "might be apt to censure such a Practice (although indeed very unjustly) as a little bordering on Cruelty. . . ." Since only the litotes keeps this statement from being a literal expression of the simple truth, the ironical negation of the parenthesis helps balance the litotes and thus helps to maintain the irony.

## CONCLUSIONS

"A Modest Proposal" is a brilliant example of the use of non-argumentative devices of rhetorical persuasion. The whole essay, of course, rests broadly upon argument of cause and effect: these causes have produced this situation in Ireland, and this proposal will result in these effects in Ireland. But Swift, within the general framework of this argument, does not employ specific argumentative forms in this essay. The projector chooses rather to *assert* his reasons and then to amass them by way of proof. He does not argue his reasons, and he does not prove them with formal arguments. In introducing the proof, the projector states that "I think the Advantages by the Proposal which I have made, are obvious, and many, as well as of the highest Importance." The fact that his reasons are "obvious" indicates that they need not be proved by argument. After having listed the sixth reason, he states that many more advantages could be "enumerated." This last word indicates that he is making no effort to prove, but merely to list. This refusal to argue his reasons is of course a persuasive device in itself, for it places the whole proposal upon the plane of obvious fact, necessary truth, rather than upon the plane of argued postulates open to debate.

Although the essay is not logically complex, it is extremely complex rhetorically—as is easily seen, for example, by the number of times in the preceding pages that a single passage has been used to demonstrate several devices which are operating at once.

Swift's ironic norm is established by the pervasive tone of diminution (human beings to animals) and by the projector's sustained point of view as an economist (his mathematics, his dealing with people as only statistical abstractions, his assuming that everyone will participate in this new industry). The human flesh is so consistently regarded as just another commodity that the whole society is finally drawn into a participation in the project—the producers, the sellers, and the consumers. This complete involvement of all classes of citizens into the scheme is arrived at by the subtle use of rhetorical devices which we have been examining—especially by the processes of diminution (for the producers) and refining (for the consumers). The norm is so thoroughly established that if the reader demurs, he will find himself to be the only one out of step.

In addition to the extensive use of these two devices of classical rhetoric, there is the fundamental ethical proof which informs the whole essay. Swift has fully exploited the possibilities of this proof by his thorough development of the character of the projector, whose personality is evident either implicitly or explicitly in every paragraph of the essay. And within these elaborately employed devices are manipulated the rhetorical devices which Swift uses less often: his direct and implied authorities; his appeal to the emotions through ocular demonstration and through the prejudices of the Irish and the Anglo-Irish; his rhetorical interrogation to allow him to assert strongly while he seems only to question mildly; his use of elimination, whereby all other proposals except his are swept aside; his uncanny use of litotes to hold the ironic pose by a single fine wire while truth is allowed to peek through for a moment; his effortless use of parenthesis to indicate whole areas of reasons which have had to be crowded out of the main line of proof; his repeatedly implied refusal to argue the "obvious." By the consummate skill with which Swift has interlocked these several devices of classical rhetoric, he has created "A Modest Proposal." To appreciate how fundamental the classical rhetoric is to the very texture of the essay, one need merely ask himself what the essay would be like if Swift had not availed himself of the long tradition of such rhetoric as it reached right down to Swift's own school days. To answer that the essay simply would not exist in its present perfection would be a conservative reply.

## CHAPTER III

# "An Argument Against Abolishing Christianity"

IN 1708 Swift went to London at the request of Archbishop King to try to get for the Irish Church what the Queen had recently granted to the English Church, the remission of the First Fruits and the twentieth parts. Initially Swift had some hope of success because his "great friends" were the Whig leaders Lord Somers and Lord Halifax. As the Whigs became less and less sympathetic toward the Church, finally endorsing the repeal of the Test Act, Swift withdrew his partial support of them and moved naturally toward support of Harley and St. John, whose views on the Church were much nearer his own. One should remember that Swift was first of all a Churchman and only secondarily a Whig or a Tory. The clearest statement of his position is his "Sentiments of a Church of England Man," written in 1708. Here he firmly declares himself to be a moderate, opposing alike the Jacobites of the extreme faction of the Tories and the "political Christians" of the Whigs.

Swift attacked these "political Christians" in 1708 by posing as one of them and writing "An ARGUMENT To prove, That the Abolishing of CHRISTIANITY IN ENGLAND, May, as Things now Stand, be attended with some Inconveniencies, and perhaps, not produce those many good Effects proposed thereby." It seems to have been prompted by Swift's growing concern over and vexation at the flagrant and sometimes vile attacks then being made upon the Church. Herbert Davis suggests that specifically Swift had in mind Tindal's *The Rights of the Christian Church, asserted against the Romish and other Priests* . . . , which Swift singles out by title in his essay and which is an attack not only upon the Church but upon the whole concept of a state-supported

establishment.[1] Swift had for a time thought to answer
Tindal with a commentary, but he turned instead to the
method of the present essay.

The irony is put immediately on a rhetorical footing, with
the opening paragraph devoted almost exclusively to ethical
proof. It is a kind of *apologia*: the author regrets that he finds
himself forced to disagree with the majority opinion, but the
good of the country demands it of him. He does not desire
to be thought presumptuous, nor does he disapprove of
state censorship on crucial topics.

I AM very sensible what a Weakness and Presumption it is,
to reason against the general Humor and Disposition of the
World. I remember it was with great Justice, and a due Regard
to the Freedom both of the Publick and the Press, forbidden
upon several Penalties to write, or discourse, or lay Wagers
against the *Union* even before it was confirmed by Parliament. . . .

Even so, he must communicate his fears to the public, although
to do so is "a manifest Breach of the Fundamental Law, that
makes this Majority of Opinion the Voice of God." He readily
admits that in committing the folly of opposing the "Current
of the People," he is no doubt the one who is out of step:
". . . I know not how, whether from the Affectation
of Singularity, or the Perverseness of human Nature; but
so it unhappily falls out, that I cannot be entirely" of the
majority opinion. Even if he were sure that "an Order were
issued out for my immediate Prosecution by the Attorney-
General; I should still confess, that in the present Posture of
our Affairs at home or abroad, I do not yet see the absolute
Necessity of extirpating the Christian Religion from among
us." He will not be dogmatic on the point; he merely does
"not yet see," implying that he is willing to be shown and
could be convinced. This idea is reinforced later by his
several statements that he is simply weighing justly the arguments on both sides; thus both sides are shown to have considerable arguments.

Implicit in the whole opening paragraph is the heroic stance
which the lone author assumes in the face of the overwhelming
majority.[2] It is a bid for immediate sympathy through the
"under-dog" appeal. Such a man, the audience feels, deserves
a hearing. This strong emotional bid for the reader's attention

and interest is of course the standard use of the classical exordium; and, although the essay does not have the regular divisions of a classical oration, it does have an exordium.

Although the author's deference is not his most pronounced personal characteristic (either genuine or for the sake of polite disputation), he manages for the most part to keep his tenacious qualities in partial check by an admirable deference. He promises that as he treats the subject, he will "handle it with all Tenderness, and with the utmost Deference to that great and profound Majority, which is of another Sentiment." These terms expressive of modesty he repeats over and over in the course of the argument: "with Deference to wiser Judgments"; "with equal Deference and Submission to wiser Judgments"; "I confess . . . (with Submission)." The same end is promoted by such expressions as "I HOPE I shall be forgiven a hard Word, if I call this a perfect Cavil."

The readiness to defer is closely allied to the author's reasonableness. Concerning the possibility that the abolition of Christianity would result in the extinction of factionalism, he states, "I CONFESS, if it were certain that so great an Advantage would redound to the Nation by this Expedient, I would submit and be silent. . . ."

Statements of the author's reasonableness heavily punctuate the essay: one such passage introduces the part of the essay devoted to the advantages and another introduces the part devoted to the disadvantages:

However, since the Undertakers propose such wonderful Advantages to the Nation by this Project; and advance many plausible Objections against the System of Christianity; I shall briefly consider the Strength of both; fairly allow them their greatest Weight, and offer such Answers as I think most reasonable. After which I will beg leave to shew what Inconveniences may possibly happen by such an Innovation, in the present Posture of our Affairs.

The reasonableness is repeated in the introduction of the second part of the essay:

HAVING thus considered the most important Objections against Christianity, and the chief Advantages proposed by the Abolishing thereof; I shall now with equal Deference and Submission to wiser Judgments as before, proceed to mention a few

Inconveniences that may happen, if the Gospel should be repealed; which perhaps the Projectors may not have sufficiently considered.

These two major statements of reasonableness and fairness are reinforced throughout the essay. In paragraph nine the author argues for the retention of Christianity on the basis that it is needed for the butt of the wits' satire, but not wishing to seem to argue from one particular to the general, he states "As to the particular Fact related, I think it is not fair to argue from one Instance; perhaps another cannot be produced. . . ." Whereupon he produces another instance to support his argument.

The author imputes anger to his opponents when they complain that there is no reason why a "Sett of Men" should be allowed "to bawl one Day in Seven" against the lawfulness of the methods most in use the other six days to gain greatness and riches. Then he chides them, "But this Objection is, I think, a little unworthy of so refined an Age as ours," and urges, "Let us argue this Matter calmly."

Proving that the spirit of opposition is much older than and independent of Christianity, the author, in a tone of utter reasonableness, once again uses the hortatory subjunctive plural: "Let us, for instance, examine wherein the Opposition of Sectaries among us consists. . . ." The frequent use of *we* and *us* tacitly assumes the mutuality of author and reader, and has the advantage of leading the reader along instead of preaching at him.

This attitude is promoted by authorial sympathy with the difficulty of the problem: ". . . I observe how difficult it is to get rid of a Phrase, which the World is once grown fond of, although the Occasion that first produced it, be entirely taken away." (The reference is to the party names drawn from religion.) Indeed, it is on this subject that the author gives the reader an autobiographical hint of his own past. He complains of "those grievous Prejudices of Education; which, under the Names of Virtue, Conscience, Honour, Justice, and the like, are so apt to disturb the Peace of human Minds; and the Notions whereof are so hard to be eradicated by right Reason, or Free-thinking, sometimes during the whole Course of our Lives." The *our* here might merely be the technique of drawing the reader to the author's side. But, since the author is probably old enough to have suffered under the old, prejudice-ridden education rather than to have enjoyed the "new Methods of Education," it is possible to see in the statement that the author himself has only lately succeeded in struggling free from the old prejudices about real religion and that he has only recently seen the true efficacy of nominal Christianity.

In such a tightly argued essay, the author is thoughtfully studious of clarity. "BUT here I would not be mistaken; and must therefore be so bold as to borrow a Distinction from the Writers on the other Side, when they make a Difference between nominal and real Trinitarians. I hope, no Reader imagines me so weak to stand up in the Defence of *real* Christianity. . . ." Again in paragraph twenty-five the author is moved to take the same caution: "I desire, I may not be mistaken; I am far from presuming to affirm or think, that the Church is in Danger at present, or as Things now stand. . . ."

Such painstaking care for clarity is further demonstrated in the author's careful checking of an argument couched in mathematics. It has been urged, he says, that "by Computation" there are above ten thousand parsons in the kingdom, whose revenues, added to those of the bishops, "would suffice to maintain, at least, two Hundred young Gentlemen of Wit and Pleasure," who would of course contribute much to both town and court. His reply contains a fine combination of several elements of the ethical proof: accuracy, concession, deference, unbiased fairness:

This, indeed, appears to be a Consideration of some Weight: But then, on the other Side, several Things deserve to be considered likewise: As, First,

whether it would not be thought necessary to have at least one man left in each parish who can read and write. But the opponent's argument fails mainly through its inherent error in the basis of the mathematics:

Then, it seems a wrong Computation, that the Revenues of the Church throughout this Island, would be large enough to maintain two Hundred young Gentlemen, or even Half that Number, after the present refined Way of Living; that is, to allow each of them such a Rent, as, in the modern Form of Speech, would make them *easy*.

We might recall the one against many of paragraph one. This stance is the most characteristic element of the ethical proof. There are at least seventeen passages in which the self-confidence of the author stands forth. His general method is to approach his argument with proper deference and an illusion of fairness, but once he has argued his way to the conclusion, he regularly chooses a bold turn of phrase to clinch his position: "It must be allowed indeed"; "Therefore, I think there is little Force in this Objection against *Christianity*"; "I think this rather shews"; the objection is "a little unworthy so refined an Age"; "To all this I answer"; "To urge another Argument"; "NOR do I think it wholly groundless"; "nothing can be more plain"; "the Reasoning they proceed by, is right"; "Perhaps I could add some others"; "notwithstanding all I have said"; "I do very much apprehend"; "nothing more manifest"; "Nothing can be more notorious"; "I am sure, few will deny."

In addition to the contribution that such strong, argumentative vocabulary makes to the ethical proof (that is, to reflect the great self-confidence of the author), it also contributes to the overwhelming illusion that the whole essay is a tightly argued performance. It is true that the essay abounds in one argumentative form after another, leading off with the first words of the title "An ARGUMENT TO PROVE. . . ." But, since Swift has his author bring forth all the wrong reasons for retaining Christianity, it is important that the argumentative tone combine with argumentative forms to create the illusion of elaborate and rock-hard argumentation.

As stated in the preceding chapter, the best ethical proof lies in a pleader's concern for the commonweal. In addition to the concern implied in undertaking the argument in the first place, there are six specific passages which reflect this highest motive for addressing oneself to his fellow citizens. In paragraph twenty-one, where the author argues that the spirit of opposition compels men to struggle over something, he states that Christianity is an excellent "Sheep-skin stuffed with Hay" to throw to the "Mastiffs" for their amusement, for

There is a Portion of Enthusiasm assigned to every Nation, which if it hath not proper Objects to work on, will burst out, and set all into a Flame. If the Quiet of a State can be bought

by only flinging Men a few Ceremonies to devour, it is a Purchase
no wise Man would refuse.

The good of the commonweal takes precedence over everything, even the existence of Christianity, and must be pur-
chased at any price, although to be sure the present price is
slight enough.

In urging that the revenues of the Church not be diverted
to the maintenance of some hundred young gentlemen of wit
and pleasure, the author appeals to the preservation of the
nation:

Now, here are ten Thousand Persons [the English clergy] reduced by the wise Regulations of *Henry* the Eighth, to the
Necessity of a low Diet, and moderate Exercise, who are the
only great Restorers of our Breed; without which, the Nation
would, in an Age or two, become but one great Hospital.

He likewise is concerned with the fair reputation of his country's wit and learning, and therefore urges the retention of
Christianity as subject matter for satire in order to prevent
"the Decline of Wit," of which "we are daily complaining."

The present ministry, which is contributing so much to the
commonweal, must not be attacked:

Great Wits love to be free with the highest Objects; and if they
cannot be allowed a *God* to revile or renounce; they will *speak
Evil of Dignities*, abuse the Government, and reflect upon the
Ministry; which I am sure, few will deny to be of much more
pernicious Consequence; according to the Saying of *Tiberius; 
Deorum offensa Diis curae*.

In the most generous concession in the essay, the author
offers to come to the aid of the projectors whom he has been
attacking, if the good of the commonweal actually necessitates
passage of the bill: "And therefore, if, notwithstanding all I
have said, it shall still be thought necessary to have a Bill
brought in for repealing Christianity," then he would humbly
offer the change of one word: instead of the word *Christianity* let the word *religion* serve in its stead. And again in
the next paragraph the author makes one final plea of similar
motivation: "UPON the whole; if it shall still be thought for
the Benefit of Church and State, that Christianity be abolished;
I conceive, however, it may be more convenient to defer the

Execution to a Time of Peace "since at the present juncture all of England's allies are Christian and "what is worse, believe a God."

The ethical proof is an important part of the rhetoric in the "Argument": in the pose of reasonableness, in the polite deference to worthier minds, in the competence and clarity of the author, in the self-confidence tempered by the show of deference, and in concern for his country. Since irony depends upon a pose or an attitude and since here as elsewhere Swift indicates his pose through a *persona*, the ethical proof is fundamental in the creation of the irony. Going far beyond its persuasive function, the ethical proof contributes to the delineation of the character of the *persona*, who is the immediate creator of the irony and who furnishes the reader a norm through which to perceive the irony and by which to measure it.

### DIMINUTION

The first seven paragraphs of the essay, down to the listing of the first advantage, serve as the introduction. These paragraphs define the argument. But while this is taking place, Swift is carefully using diminution of terms to lift the matter of the debate from its deep fundamentals to the surface of words only.

The opening sentence sets up an opposition which continues through the whole essay: the author acknowledges it a weakness "to reason" against the "general Humor and Disposition of the World." He is going against that "fundamental Law, that makes this Majority of Opinion the Voice of God." On his side stands the word *reason*; on the world's side stand *humour*, *disposition*, and *opinion*. In the next paragraph he adds to this list the word *sentiment*: he will defend Christianity "with all Tenderness, and with the utmost Deference to that great and profound Majority, which is of another Sentiment."

But this strong dichotomy of terms is not insisted upon: the word *reason* occurs only once; the other terms just named give the two opening paragraphs their prevailing tone. Having set this tone of *opinion* and *humor* as the correct terms for the majority, he sets about to reduce the Christian side to the neutral position of being sentiment instead of fact. He lays

the ground-work for this in paragraph three and then makes
his point explicit in paragraph five, where he reduces the whole
debate to one of nominalism.

In paragraph three he comments upon the fadism of
opinion. There are, he says, some old people who can still
remember when it was just as popular to defend Christianity
as it is now to attack it:

> AND yet the Curious may please to observe, how much the
> Genius of a Nation is liable to alter in half an Age: I have heard
> it affirmed for certain by some very old People, that the contrary
> Opinion was even in their Memories as much in vogue as the
> other is now; and, that a Project for the Abolishing of Chris-
> tianity would then have appeared as singular, and been thought
> as absurd, as it would be at this Time to write or discourse in
> its Defence.

Having reduced religious principles to nothing more than fads,
he at the same time reduces movements against them to nothing
more than projects. And there were, of course, enough hair-
brained projects being circulated to render all such proposals
suspect. Thus the present essay becomes a plea to examine all
the implications of a project the main point of which might
be deceptively efficacious. This paragraph thus is the opening
step leading to the nominalism of paragraph five, but characteristically Swift does not move immediately to his final
position. Paragraph four simply amplifies paragraph three.
Having levelled the majority to the plane of opinion, he
reduces the Christian religion to merely one of several dead
systems: "The System of the Gospel, after the Fate of other
Systems is generally antiquated and exploded. . . ." Even the
commonalty are as much ashamed of it as "their Betters" are:
"Opinions, like Fashions always descending from those of
Quality to the middle Sort, and thence to the Vulgar, where
at length they are dropt and vanish."

Thus in a brief space Swift reduces the belief of the
majority first to opinion and then to a mere fashion, at the
same time reducing Christianity from the true religion to only
one of several dead systems. He is now ready to reduce the
terms of the argument and the argument itself to sheer nominalism. In the opening sentence of paragraph four, he admitted
that "all Appearances are against me." In context the word

*appearances* implies the idea that *apparently* he is arguing at a disadvantage. But he has planted the word in the reader's mind. And now in paragraph five the pattern is extended:

BUT here I would not be mistaken; and must therefore be so bold as to borrow a Distinction from the Writers on the other Side, when they make a Difference between nominal and real *Trinitarians*. I hope, no Reader imagines me so weak to stand up in the Defence of *real* Christianity; such as used in primitive Times (if we may believe the Authors of those Ages) to have an Influence upon Mens Belief and Actions: To offer at the Restoring of that, would indeed be a wild Project; it would be to dig up Foundations; to destroy at one Blow *all* the Wit, and *half* the Learning of the Kingdom; to break the entire Frame and Constitution of Things; to ruin Trade, extinguish Arts and Sciences with the Professors of them; in short, to turn our Courts, Exchanges and Shops into Desarts. . . .

To restore *real* Christianity would be to dig up foundations. The question however is *nominal*, dealing only with appearances. The whole argument has thus been moved from the plane of fundamentals to the surface plane, the plane of nominals. The point is thus ironically made that much of the religious and party struggle is not in fact based upon religious principle.

Fearing, possibly, that this paragraph was too strong, with a characteristic undercutting which is devastating, Swift hastens to add that the contents of the whole paragraph are only a "Caution" which is "in itself altogether unnecessary, (which I have inserted to prevent all possibility of cavilling) since every candid Reader will easily understand my Discourse to be intended only in Defence of *nominal* Christianity. . . ."

In paragraph seven, the last of the introductory section, Swift has arrived at the definition of the subject (to examine the reasons for and against abolishing nominal Christianity) through a combination of two sets of diminution: one diminishing the position of the majority; the other diminishing the Christian position. The final step in the diminution to nominalism is made in paragraph seven: the argument reduces itself to whether the *name* "Christian" should be retained:

BUT why we should therefore cast off the Name and Title of Christian, although the general Opinion and Resolution be so violent for it; I confess I cannot (with Submission) apprehend the Consequence necessary.

In addition to the use of this particular line of diminution throughout the essay, the device occurs in its fullest form in one of the major arguments of the essay. In paragraph fifteen the author refutes the contention that the abolition of Christianity will completely extinguish party distinctions and conflicts (High and Low Church, Whig, Tory, etc.). This, he says, is patently false. The spirit of party strife and opposition ("that one darling Inclination of Mankind") is innate and will not be removed with the removal of Christianity. Christianity has merely offered in its brief time the phrases which name opposing factions, which could just as easily find new appellations for themselves:

Because Religion was nearest at Hand to furnish a few convenient Phrases; is our Invention so barren, we can find no others? Suppose, for Argument Sake, that the *Tories* favoured *Margarita*, the *Whigs* Mrs. *Tofts*, and the *Trimmers Valentini;* would not *Margaritians*, *Toftians*, and *Valentinians*, be very tolerable Marks of Distinction? [These three ladies were singers of Italian opera in London.]

Swift gives the argument for nominalism a semblance of reality by citing a similarly pointless naming of parties in the Rome of Justinian, where the parties were named for the colors of the ribbons worn by racing horses:

The *Prasini* and *Veneti*, two most virulent Factions in *Italy*, began (if I remember right) by a Distinction of Colours in Ribbonds; which we might do, with as good Grace, about the Dignity of the *Blue* and the *Green;* and would serve as properly to divide the Court, the Parliament, and the Kingdom between them, as any Terms of Art whatsover, borrowed from Religion. [These two parties—the Green and the Blue, respectively—caused the civil war in Justinian's reign.]

The author pursues the same idea with even more examples. ". . . if the Words *Whoring, Drinking, Cheating, Lying, Stealing*, were, by Act of Parliament, ejected out of the *English* Tongue and Dictionaries," would we awake the next day "chaste and temperate"? No, he answers. Would the removal of the names of certain diseases result in the extinction of those diseases? Again, no. "Are Envy, Pride, Avarice and Ambition, such ill Nomenclators, that they can not furnish Appellations for their Owners? Will not *Heydukes* and *Mamalukes, Mandarins,* and *Potshaws,* or any other Words formed at Pleasure, serve to distinguish those who are in the *Ministry* from others, who *would be in* it *if they could?*" The point is proved: Christianity just happened to have been the source of terms for naming the factions. In reality the only important distinction is who is in power and who is out. Swift's satiric point is well taken here, for in many of the *Examiner Papers* he argues that both Whig and Tory agree to the fundamentals of the English Constitution and disagree only in means. Only pride and avarice of party members cause bitter factionalism and slanderous accusations and appellations of disloyalty.[3]

Whereas in "A Modest Proposal" Swift kept diminution operating at a plane behind the argument, but pervading it, he has here brought diminution into play with the actual argument, in the example just discussed and in the statement of the subject of the whole essay (paragraph 1).

Once the subject has been defined as "nominal Christianity," this phrase continues for the rest of the essay: "*nominal* Religion"; "*nominal* Faith"; the argument proving nominalism, just discussed; "BUT why we should cast off the Name and Title of Christians"; "*Nominal* Christianity." The author fears that the "Execution" should be postponed until a time of peace because, "as it falls out," England's allies are all Christians and might be disobliged. In fact, many of them "by the Prejudices of their Education, [are] so bigotted, as to place a Sort of Pride in the Appellation." Indeed, they "are not only strict Observers of religious Worship; but, what is worse, believe a God; which is more than is required of us, even while we preserve the Name of Christians."

This nominalism, having been sustained almost to the end of the essay, is brought powerfully into play at the very end, where it once again functions as an argument. Having convinced the reader that the whole argument is in reality based upon nominalism, Swift in a brilliant stroke uses this very surface device to plunge into the heart of the question. In paragraph twenty-seven, after having discussed the advantages and objections, he slips in one slight but devastating sugges-

tion. If it still be thought necessary, he says, to bring in a bill
to abolish Christianity, then he would "humbly offer an
Amendment, That instead of the Word *Christianity*, may be
put *Religion* in general, which I conceive, will much better
answer all the good Ends proposed by the Projectors of it."
Swift has so carefully managed the diminution to nominalism
that at the point in the essay in which he wishes to make
his strongest ironic attack, he has merely to keep his pose as
a dealer in words and simply offer the substitution of one single
word for another.

The whole use of diminution to nominalism is the major
function of the device in this essay, for in addition to its
role of helping to set the general tone and vocabulary of
the essay, it functions within specific arguments themselves.

Other diminution operates as the device does in "A Modest
Proposal," creating the milieu of the essay and reflecting the
society for which it is written. Diminution is employed in the
following categories: priests; the Church; the classical, religious
education formerly obtainable at the universities; the Christian position; and the freethinkers.

In paragraph seven, after having promised a fair weighing
of the reasons for and against the abolition, the author states,
"After which I will beg leave to shew what Inconveniences
may possibly happen by such an Innovation, in the present
Posture of our Affairs."

The consequences of abolishing Christianity are merely
"Inconveniences" which may "possibly" result. But the project
to abolish it is an "Innovation." The first advantage for
the proposal is that it would very much "enlarge and establish Liberty of Conscience, that great Bulwark of our Nation, and of the *Protestant* Religion, which is too much limited
by *Priest-craft* . . . ."

The priests of the Established Church are seldom so named.
Rather they are "daggled-tail Parsons." Parson is a "coun-
trified" name, less elegant than *minister*.[4] They are potential
"Recruits" for the army and the fleet in the event Christianity
is abolished. They are twice called the perpetrators of "*Priest-
Craft*." They are a "Sett of Men" who are suffered to "bawl
One Day in Seven, against the Lawfulness of those Methods
most in Use towards the Pursuit of Greatness, Riches, and

Pleasure; which are the constant Practice of all Men alive on the other Six." Although he uses the word *Sunday* elsewhere, he twice substitutes the secular periphrasis "one Day in Seven." The priests are "Objects of Scorn and Contempt" which men of wit must have for their subject matter. Parishes become "certain Tracts of Country," and the church buildings are "stately Structures now in the Hands of the Clergy" which, when the proposed bill is passed, can easily be converted into "Play-houses, Exchanges, Market-houses, common Dormitories, and other publick Edifices."

Closely associated with the diminution of the clergy and the Church is the diminution of the classical and religious education which during the Christian era was offered at the Universities. But this education is now out of favor.

IT is likewise proposed, as a great Advantage to the Publick, that if we once discard the System of the Gospel, all Religion will, of Course, be banished for ever; and consequently along with it, those grievous prejudices of Education; which, under the Names of Virtue, Conscience, Honour, Justice, and the like, are so apt to disturb the Peace of human Minds; and the Notions whereof are so hard to be eradicated by right Reason, or Free-Thinking, sometimes during the whole Course of our Lives.

The old education is referred to as the "Prejudices of their Education," as "Pedantry," "Fountain" of outmoded education from which were "said to be derived all our foolish Notions of Justice, Piety, Love of our Country; all our Opinions of God, or a future State, Heaven, Hell, and the like. . . ."

But so effectual Care hath been since taken, to remove those Prejudices by an entire Change in the Methods of Education; that (with Honour I mention it to our polite Innovators) the young Gentlemen, who are now on the Scene, seem to have not the least Tincture left of those Infusions, or String of those Weeds. . . .

The two young men who proved the nonexistence of God and who so "generously" communicated their thoughts to the world accomplished this great feat "by the meer Force of natural Abilities, without the least Tincture of Learning. . . ."

The three areas of diminution just discussed contribute

to the largest single diminution in the essay: the use of the lesser word in naming the Christian position. The diminution becomes even more pointed when it is realized that it is redoubled: the less word is used to replace "nominal Christianity," which is the diminished form of "real Christianity."

In the discussion of nominalism, it was observed that Christianity was merely one of several dead "Systems." It is "The System of the Gospel," "System of Christianity," "Gospel System." It is "narrow Principles" and "Prejudices." When the author answers the objection that "the Gospel System . . . obliges Men to the Belief of Things too difficult for Free-Thinkers," he answers, "Does any Man either believe, or say he believes, or desire to have it thought that he says he believes one Syllable of the Matter?" Religion has degenerated to mere "Notions of Religion," and the author objects that he does not believe for a moment that religion is the "Invention of Politicians" intended to keep the common people in awe, although "I can conceive some scattered *Notions* about a superior Power to be of singular Use for the Common People, as furnishing excellent Materials to keep Children quiet when they grow peevish, and providing Topicks of Amusement in a tedious Winter Night."

When the author defends Christianity from the charge that it causes the "Opposition of Sectaries," he points out that the "Spirit of Opposition" is much older than Christianity and that it can exist without Christianity. However, "if Christianity did not lend its Name to stand in the Gap," this enthusiasm would be turned full on the laws of the land and disturb the public peace, for every nation has a certain share of enthusiasm, and if it does not have "proper Objects to work on, it will set all into a flame." Christianity is such an "Object"; it is a "Purchase no wise Man would refuse." In so many words, then, Christianity is diminished to a tub which is thrown to divert a whale. If Christianity were not put to this use, "the Legislature must find *some other Expedient* to employ and entertain" the sectaries.

Not only is Christianity a topic of amusement for winter nights and a material for putting fear into obstreperous children, but also it is the main stock of learned men. The author, remarking on "the great Decline of Wit among us," asks "would we take away the greatest, perhaps the only Topick we have left," Christianity? "Who would ever have suspected *Asgill* for a Wit, or *Toland* for a Philosopher, if the inexhaustible *Stock* of Christianity had not been at hand to provide them with *Materials?*"

But all of the diminution is not directed against the Christian side of the argument; the author is after all defending Christianity from the attack being make upon it by certain projectors. While the author evidently does not use the word *projector* disparagingly, Swift clearly does. The author is attacking this particular project, not all projects. The men who have proposed the bill to abolish Christianity are "Projectors," "Undertakers"; their proposal is a "Project," an "Innovation," an "Expedient," and a "Scheme."[5]

The author's middle position gives him opponents on either hand: "*Atheists, Deists, Socinians, Anti-Trinitarians,* and other Subdivisions of Free-Thinkers" are on the one side, and, on the other, Dissenters and Presbyterians, who, although Christian, oppose the Establishment. Diminution is employed against both groups. The Gospel "obliges men to the Belief of Things too difficult for Free-Thinkers." The writings of the deists Asgill, Tindall, Toland, and Coward is "Trumpery," which gets a hearing only because it is on the popular subject of attacking Christianity. This is more specifically name-calling, the frankest species of diminution.

The projectors' bill is no more than the first "political Step" in a move to abolish the Establishment. Some of their arguments are mere pretences and pretexts. The writings of the men of wit are "scrophulous consumptive Productions." This attack through diminution on men whom the author apparently admires presents an ambiguity, for the author devotes much of his amplification to these same persons.

## AMPLIFICATION

In order better to understand Swift's use of amplification[6] in this essay, it is helpful to determine as nearly as possible the exact position which his author assumes with reference to the argument. Swift's position is clear enough, but not so his author's. The author is a nominal Christian who understands the advantages of retaining this nominal religion. To that

extent he is sympathetic toward the freethinkers. Thus his
pro-freethinking statements are intended praise, even though
he is not himself one of the number of "*Atheists, Deists,
Socinians, Anti-Trinitarians,* and other Sub-divisions of Free-
Thinkers." He firmly believes in the Establishment, and
therefore the Roman Catholics and Presbyterians are his
enemies. The freethinkers become his enemies only when they
move to threaten the Establishment itself. Otherwise, the
author admires their progressive liberalism. Much confusion
concerning the amplification is thus dispelled when it is borne
in mind that the author has been caught up in the freethinking
current and can only occasionally perceive the freethinkers as
his real enemy. His ambivalent attitude toward the freethinkers
accounts for his praise of the world through freethinking
jargon and also for his few strong attacks upon the free-
thinkers.

The author has had some education. He is an artful and
determined disputant, and he seems abreast of current polemical
writing. But he probably has only recently come up to town
and even more recently fallen into muddled freethinking logic.
He has not completely succeeded in extricating himself from
his old training in real Christianity, for at one point in the
essay he laments that that cannot be accomplished "sometimes
during the whole Course of our Lives." A further indication
that he is an older person who is not quite at home with
"modern living" occurs in paragraph eleven, where he reckons
that the Church revenues will be insufficient to maintain some
hundred young gentlemen of wit: he seems not to know personally about "the present refined Way of Living," and he
apologizes for using a new phrase: "as, in the modern Form
of Speech, would make them *easy*."

Since amplification, either real or ironic, rests upon a value
system, this background on the author makes it possible to
define the point of view informing the amplification. The
following are the main areas of amplification in the essay:
the polite world and men of wit, pleasure, and learning; free-
thinking; wisdom and rationalism (especially reasoning not
"tainted" with the old education); reformers and wise projectors; the new education. Swift withholds any amplification
until paragraph eight, at which point he introduces in a single

paragraph all of the areas of amplification which he will subsequently weave in and out of the essay, just as a composer might open with a full-chord statement before beginning the variations. I shall quote the paragraph in full:

First, ONE great Advantage proposed by the Abolishing of Christianity is, That it would very much enlarge and establish Liberty of Conscience, that great Bulwark of our Nation, and of the *Protestant* Religion, which is still too much limited by *Priest-Craft*, notwithstanding all the good Intentions of the Legislature; as we have lately found by a severe Instance. For it is confidently reported, that two young Gentlemen of great Hopes, bright Wit, and profound Judgment, who upon a thorough Examination of Causes and Effects, and by the meer Force of natural Abilities, without the least Tincture of Learning; having made a Discovery, that there was no God, and generously communicating their Thoughts for the Good of the Publick; were some Time ago, by an unparalleled Severity, and upon I know not what *obsolete* Law, broke only for *Blasphemy*. And as it hath been wisely observed; if Persecution once begins, no Man alive knows how far it may reach, or where it will end.

In the next paragraph the author urges the retention of nominal Christianity for the "great Wits," who have ever needed God to be a butt for their wit. "Blasphemy we know is freely spoke a Million of Times in every Coffeehouse and Tavern, or wherever else *good Company* meet."

The author acknowledges that "Gentlemen of Wit and Pleasure" are likely to be offended by so many "daggled-tail Parsons"; however, he answers that the "wise Reformers" have not sufficiently considered in this instance that these persons are perfect butts for the gentlemen's literary productions. Only upon such an object can "great Wits" practice and improve their talents. Likewise for the freethinkers and polemicists: ". . . how could the Freethinkers, the strong Reasoners, and the Men of profound Learning be able to find another Subject so calculated in all Points whereon to display their Abilities?"

The wisdom of the polite world and indeed of the whole nation is used to buttress the author's answer to the second objection to nominal Christianity (that this religion obliges men to believe things too difficult to accept): "To which I

answer, that Men should be cautious how they raise Objections, which reflect upon the Wisdom of the Nation." He
dismisses the foolish notion that belief is involved, affirming
that verbal acceptance is the only requirement. In paragraph
nineteen the author is even more explicit in indicating that
almost the whole population of England is praiseworthy for
its liberal freethinking: ". . . For I look upon the Mass, or
Body of our People here in *England*, to be as Free-thinkers,
that is to say, as staunch Unbelievers, as any of the highest
Rank." Thus, this great quality of the polite world has per-
colated down through the whole society.

Added to this implicit praise for the whole society's opinion
is the blanket labeling of this opinion as "right": "Is not every
Body freely allowed to believe whatever he thinks fit, especially if it serves to strengthen the Party which is in the
Right?" The author's equating *might* and *right* in this amplification further indicates his value-system.

". . . two Hundred young Gentlemen of Wit and Pleasure,
and Freethinking; Enemies to Priest-craft, narrow Principles,
Pedantry and Prejudices" could be kept as "an Ornament
to the Court and Town" if the Church revenues could be
diverted to their up-keep. "The Men of Pleasure" make
perfectly good uses of the seventh day; thus there is no need
to abolish Christianity in order to gain one day more per week
for business and pleasure. The objection that preachers should
not be allowed "to bawl" at men one day in seven "is, I think,
a little unworthy so refined an Age as ours." "I appeal to the
breast of any polite Free-thinker" to know whether he is
really hindered from business and pleasure by the Sabbath.

The banishment of the "System of the Gospel" will,
it is urged, get rid of all religion, and "consequently along
with it, those grievous Prejudices of Education" such as
virtue, conscience, honor, justice. But, an "entire Change in
the Methods of Education" has already done away with the
old virtues, thus obviating this whole objection.

The final argument in favor of abolishing Christianity is
that the abolition will greatly enlarge the terms of communion
and broaden the basis of the Establishment by "opening a
large and noble Gate" to replace the "few Wickets" now
being opened to allow entry of a few chaffering dissenters.

This passage is a variation of the amplification of the polite, learned world which wants a "noble Gate" and not the old-fashioned "wickets."

It will be noticed that almost all of the examples of amplification cited above are verbal amplification but that some employ amplification of point of view rather than of word. I have included this second kind in order to indicate the broader use to which Swift has put this device in this essay. Not only does he use simple verbal amplification, but also he establishes the inverted values of the polite and witty world as the satiric norm for the essay. This broader use of amplification is thus a basic rhetorical device in the essay, establishing as it does through the pervasive effect of vocabulary the point of view of the polite word as the "right" one. From the point of view of rhetorical argument, Swift is using the technique of convicting his opponents out of their own mouths, of assuming their point of view and of arguing rampantly with their questionable opinions and logic.

I have suggested that the author admires and aspires to this polite world but that he does not as yet feel himself a part of it, that he has accepted its value-system but that he only occasionally perceives that the body of freethinkers is actually an enemy to the Establishment. He is in the predicament of the liberal who keeps discovering liberal viewpoints which he cannot accept. It is this ambivalence which for the most part accounts for the few occasions when the author turns on the freethinkers an acid sarcasm inconsistent with the general tone of amplification. There are four such passages which apparently are inconsistent with the amplification, and they are crucial because they raise the question of whether Swift has broken the ironic pose. In an irony of inversion the author must at some time "tip his hand" and remove enough layers of the irony to indicate his real position on the matter in hand. In the preceding chapter it was demonstrated that Swift held his pose perfectly, that at the few points where he raised the ironic curtain, he brought into play other rhetorical devices sufficient to maintain the smooth ironic pose of the very surface. But, in the present essay, when the author labels as "Trumpery" the writings of the deists "*Asgill, Tindall, Toland, Coward,*" does he break through his pose? That is, does he tip his hand too obviously? In paragraph eleven, when the author argues that a few priests should be retained so that at least one man in each parish would be literate, he breaks out in an attack on the young men of wit and pleasure in the most savage language of the essay:

For, pray, what would become of the Race of Men in the next Age, if we had nothing to trust to, besides the scrophulous consumptive Productions furnished by our Men of Wit and Pleasure; when having squandered away their Vigour, Health, and Estates; they are forced, by some disagreeable Marriage, to piece up their broken Fortunes, and entail Rottenness and Politeness on their Posterity? Now, here are ten thousand Persons reduced, by the wise Regulations of *Henry* the Eighth, to the necessity of a low Diet, and moderate Exercise, who are the only great Restorers of our Breed; without which, the Nation would, in an Age or two, become but one great Hospital.

In arguing that religion is needed as subject matter upon which great wits can show their talents, the author asks, "Who would ever have suspected *Asgill* for a Wit, or *Toland* for a Philosopher, if the inexhaustible Stock of Christianity had not been at hand to provide them with Materials? What other Subject through all Art or Nature could have produced *Tindal* for a profound Author, or furnished him with Readers?"

Do these three separate passages constitute a rupture of the ironic pose?[7] Possibly the most realistic answer is yes, that Swift simply failed to contain his contempt. The Christianity essay is second only to "A Modest Proposal" as an essay of ironic inversion; and, if we are justified in praising Swift so highly for his uncanny ability to maintain a pose perfectly and to keep the surface of his ironical essays completely smooth and unmarred, how then is it reasonable to impute to him so gross a flaw in this essay? If dramatic consistency is demanded on the mechanical level of irony, I suggest that Swift is following his penchant for parody and that he quite deliberately has bestowed upon his author this muddle-headedness arising from the author's ambivalent attitude of admiration and disgust towards men of wit, pleasure, and learning. However, when a writer elects to objectify his composition by writing through a *persona*, it is always easy and sometimes glib for one to attribute any flaws to that *persona* rather than to its creator.

To insist, however, that good irony always must sustain an unmarred pose at the surface is to reason narrowly, for Swift himself is proof against the contention. In these examples from the Christianity essay, I have indicated that the break-throughs can be rationalized for the sake of ironic "art," but elsewhere Swift has other such break-throughs which cannot be so "explained." In "The Answer to the *Craftsman*" he carefully builds diminution with the ironically appropriate terms until at the very end of the essay he bursts forth frankly calling the Irish "Slaves." In *Examiner* No. 17 he set out to attack Lord Wharton by imitating Cicero's first oration against Verres, but after continuing long enough to make his point, Swift breaks off: "THIS Extract, to deal ingenuously, hath cost me more Pains than I think it is worth, having only served to convince me, that modern Corruptions are not to be paralleled by ancient Examples, without having recourse to Poetry or Fable." In "A Short View of the State of Ireland," a non-ironic essay, Swift begins an ironic passage in which he describes the wonderfully prosperous condition of Ireland, but after two brief paragraphs, he confesses that he cannot go on: "But my Heart is too heavy to continue this Irony longer; for it is manifest, that whatever Stranger took such a Journey, would be apt to think himself travelling in *Lapland*, or *Ysland*, rather than in a Country so favoured by Nature as ours, both in Fruitfulness of Soil, and Temperature of Climate." Such personal break-throughs are powerful and exciting. They are not blunders; they are adroitly calculated to be impassioned over-flowings through which Swift faces his reader directly and indicates that there are limits to the rules of ironic art which must be laid aside when, for the moment, they have been exhausted. Swift's break-throughs are not accidental "lapses" in which he personally cannot contain his indignation. They are rhetorical and are designed to communicate powerfully that the superlative of the matter being treated has been reached. And, in the essays of complete ironic inversion which are written by a *persona*, these eruptions give the added dimension resulting from the presence of both the ironist and his creature.

## THE APPEAL TO AUTHORITY

The appeal to authority in this essay is of two kinds: establishing a point of view as the one generally held and consented to by the majority of citizens, and what might be described as the appeal to non-specific authority. If we grant that the author's quoting Tacitus in paragraph nine is an appeal to a specific authority, then it can be said that there is one appeal to direct authority. However, this use of Tacitus seems rather to be an argument by proverb, in which case then there is not a single appeal to a specific authority. Rather, unstated authorities and uncited sources supply the basis of the appeal.

In paragraph sixteen the author states, "I appeal to the Breast of any polite Free-Thinker, whether in the Pursuit of gratifying a predominant Passion, he hath not always felt a wonderful Incitement, by reflecting it was a Thing forbidden. . . ." In charging that this bill is only the first step towards setting up Presbytery as the Establishment, he states that we will leave this "to be further considered by those at the Helm." Possibly the ministry are a kind of authority to which the question can vaguely but confidently be referred. However, most of these appeals are even more vague. Their grammatical construction is the key to them: without exception they are expressed by agentless passive voice verbs: "It is confidently reported"; "It is likewise urged"; "as I am told"; "From this Fountain were said to be derived"; "It is so recorded."

In paragraph twenty-five the author appeals to common knowledge, which although general is a justified generality: "*Nothing can be more notorious* than that the *Atheists, Deists, Socinians, Anti-Trinitarians,* and other Subdivisions of Free-Thinkers, are Persons of little Zeal for the present Ecclesiastical Establishment: Their declared Opinion is for repealing the sacramental Test . . . ."

In the two closing pleas of the essay occur two concessions to some authority: "if it still be thought necessary to have a Bill brought in for repealing Christianity" and "if it should still be thought for the Benefit of Church and State." Whoever is the actor of these two verbs of thinking has sufficient power and wisdom to decide that Christianity should be abolished. Here again the author defers to the opinion of the majority.

In addition to the passive voice verbs just discussed, there are many others which are used to introduce the various advantages and disadvantages, as in " 'Tis proposed as a singular Advantage."

Why has Swift kept his authorities general and vague? Professor Davis has suggested that Swift seems to have considered answering Tindal's *The Rights of the Christian Church* with a non-ironical rebuttal but that he wrote the "Argument" instead. To have answered Tindal would have been to answer only one man. By treating his opponents only in the abstract, Swift could thus attack the whole anti-religious and anti-Establishment climate at once. He answers not one opponent, but all *"Atheists, Deists, Socinians, Anti-Trinitarians," "Asgill, Tindall, Toland, Coward,* and Forty more." In addition, therefore, to the purely rhetorical effect of keeping the enemy vague, weak, and unreal through this faceless abstraction, Swift also indicates the scope and aim of his ironic attack: the whole climate of opinion.

By far the more fundamental use of appeal to authority is the author's tacit assumption underlying almost every paragraph that all England has long ago completely accepted nominal Christianity over real Christianity. Such an assumption allows the author to appeal to this authority at random and even to use the majority opinion as the basis of an argument. This technique serves several rhetorical purposes. It places the reader and the author on somewhat intimate grounds of common agreement, since they have agreed on terms and the religious situation and disagree only on the efficacy of the present bill under consideration. It allows the author to gain sympathy for himself by opposing the majority opinion at the same time that he is assuming as true the majority's belief in nominal Christianity. And, lastly, it combines with the diminution of the Church side to establish both implicitly and explicitly the satiric norm.

The author states that it is the "general Humour and Disposition of the World" to abolish Christianity; it is the "Current of the People"; the author speaks out at a juncture "when all Parties appear so unanimously determined upon the Point;

as we cannot but allow from their Actions, their Discourses, and their Writings." In the second paragraph the author promises to treat gently "the profound Majority." He states that he knows some "very old People" who can still recall when it would have been just as absurd to attack Christianity "as it would be at this Time to write or discourse in its Defence." "The System of the Gospel, after the Fate of other Systems is generally antiquated and exploded; and the Mass or Body of the common People, among whom it seems to have had its latest Credit, are now grown as much ashamed of it as their Betters."

The tone of the following sentence indicates the majority opinion: "I hope, no Reader imagines me so weak to stand up in the Defence of *real* Christianity. . . . To offer at the Restoring of that, would indeed be a wild Project . . . ." And even to make this distinction has been an "unnecessary" "Caution" inserted only to prevent "all possibility of cavilling, since every candid Reader will easily understand my Discourse to be intended only in Defence of *nominal* Christianity; the other having been for some time wholly laid aside by general Consent, as utterly inconsistent with all our present Schemes of Wealth and Power." In paragraph seven the author is at a loss to understand why "the general Opinion and Resolution" be so violent for casting off even "the Name and Title of Christians."

Opinion of the members of Parliament also reflects the general climate: the liberty of conscience is "still too much limited by *Priest-Craft*, notwithstanding all the good Intentions of the Legislature; as we have lately found by a severe Instance."

Some men have argued, the author states, that "the Gospel System" requires men to believe "Things too difficult for Free-Thinkers, and such who have shook off the Prejudices that usually cling to a confined Education. To which I answer, that Men should be cautious how they raise Objections, which reflect upon the Wisdom of the Nation." This statement is followed by a long series of rhetorical questions, the answers to which are all predicated upon the majority opinion.

Another advantage proposed by the abolition of Christianity "is the clear Gain of one Day in seven" which could be used for secular purposes. But, the author argues, no man now living seems remotely hindered from conducting all manner of business and pleasure on Sunday, for it is the implicit opinion of the nation that men can gamble at home at least one day of the week instead of at the Chocolate-House, that traders tally their account books each Sunday, that lawyers prepare the next week's briefs each Sunday, etc.

The author states that preachers rail against "the Lawfulness of those Methods most in Use towards the Pursuit of Greatness, Riches and Pleasure; which are the constant Practice of all Men alive on the other Six." In the final paragraph the author points out the patent contradiction of spending more money to destroy Christianity "than ever the Wisdom of our Age thought fit to venture for the *Preservation* of Christianity."

The constant and even tone of these assumptions of common opinion serves two purposes: it contributes fundamentally to the satiric norm, and it serves in some of the major arguments. It functions as the chorus for the satiric setting of the essay, and occasionally comes downstage to participate in the actual action.

## THE RHETORICAL QUESTION

The essay against abolishing Christianity abounds in rhetorical argument. However, Swift has used several tricks of rhetoric to make it appear to be more "reasoned" than it actually is. As has been noticed already, Swift, beginning with the very first word of the title "AN ARGUMENT To prove. . . ," has cast over the essay a vocabulary which helps create an illusion of elaborate argumentation—elaborate in the sense that even a close reading of the essay gives one the impression that he has been hit hard and rapidly and repeatedly with a great flow of persuasive arguments. But an examination of these "arguments" reveals that many of them are not formal arguments at all, that Swift has employed non-argumentative devices to a much greater extent than the total impression of the essay would seem to suggest.

There are twelve "arguments" dealt with: eight are for abolition and four are against. Let us briefly examine these.

For abolition:

1.   Abolition would enlarge liberty of conscience:
      Swift answers by arguing from consequences.
      Great wits must have a butt for their wit and
Argument   satire. If it were not Christianity, they might
      actually turn on the government and ministry,
      the result of which would prove to be much
      more pernicious.

2.   The Gospel system requires belief of things too
      difficult for some men:
No argument Swift uses a rhetorical question to nullify the
      issue.

3.   Church monies could be used to maintain 200
      gentlemen of wit and pleasure:
      Swift answers with counter arguments: at
      least one literate man is needed in each parish;
Both    Christianity furnishes the needed butt for the
      wits. Between these two answers, he slips in
      a nullification of the proposed reason by show-
      ing that there is insufficient money anyway.

4.   Abolition would result in the gain of one day in
      seven:
No argument Rhetorical question nullifies the contention.

5.   Abolition would remove party strife:
Both    Nullified by rhetorical question and then
      argued against through redefinition of terms.

6.   A set of men should not be able to bawl against
      accepted schemes of pleasure and business:
Argument   Swift argues that prohibition ever enhances
      sin.

7.   Prejudices of old religion would be removed:
      Swift nullifies the question: the new educa-
No argument tion has already accomplished this for the
      polite world, and the vulgar have long since
      followed their betters.

8.   Abolition would enlarge the basis of the Establish-
      ment:
      Swift answers with the argument that the
Argument   spirit of opposition is older than and not in-
      tegral to Christiantiy. He argues through
      clarification of terms, and re-definition.

Against abolition:
  9. Argument   Great wits need parsons for butts.
 10. Argument   Free thinkers need Christianity as a butt.
 11. Argument   The Establishment might be endangered by
               the Presbyterians and the Papists.
 12. Argument   Removing Christianity might force the people
               to superstition, most assuredly to Roman Cath-
               olic superstitions.

Of these twelve "arguments" seven are argued (1, 6, 8, 9,
10, 11, 12), three are destroyed without argument (2, 4, 7),
and two are argued even though the questions are first nullified (3, 5). After the seven-paragraph introduction there
follows the largest unit of the essay, the fifteen-paragraph
section given over to the answering of the arguments in favor
of the abolition. This is followed by a heavy pause at paragraph twenty-two, in which the author introduces the second
section of the essay. This section, containing the four arguments against abolition, is contained in only four paragraphs.
The conclusion follows, beginning at paragraph twenty-seven.
For emphasis and power for the positive side of the question,
the author uses only argument for his second section. These
four arguments follow each other succinctly in rapid order.

Isolating for a moment the section against abolition, one
is struck most forcibly with the non-argued aspects of the
essay. There are eight arguments in this section; two are nullified and three are dismissed with rhetorical questions.

The second reason for the abolition is that the Gospel
system "requires men to the Belief of Things too difficult for
Free-Thinkers, and such who have shook off the Prejudices
that usually cling to a confined Education." The author, not
deigning to dignify this assertion with a formal answer, counters with an extended series of rhetorical questions. He seems
further to show his contempt by allowing his questions merely
to dangle, for at the end of the last question he concludes the
paragraph and in the next paragraph turns to an entirely new
consideration.

Is not every Body freely allowed to believe whatever he pleaseth;
and to publish his Belief to the World whenever he thinks fit;

especially if it serve to strengthen the Party which is in the Right? Would any indifferent Foreigner, who should read the Trumpery lately written by *Asgill, Tindall, Toland, Coward,* and Forty more, imagine the Gospel to be our Rule of Faith, and confirmed by Parliaments? Does any Man either believe, or say he believes, or desire to have it thought that he says he believes one Syllable of the Matter? And is any Man worse received upon that Score; or does he find his Want of *Nominal* Faith a Disadvantage to him, in the Pursuit of any Civil, or Military Employment? What if there be an old dormant Statute or two against him? Are they not now obsolete, to a Degree, that *Empson* and *Dudley* themselves, if they were now alive, would find it impossible to put them in Execution?

Turning immediately to the contention that Church revenues could be used to support two hundred men of wit and pleasure, the author counters that at least one literate man is needed in each parish. But then he completely obviates the question with the statement that all of the Church monies would prove insufficient for this new use. Then, as if to beat the dog which is already dead, he returns with a further argument that Christianity is necessary to serve as the object of the gentlemen's wit and scorn.

In the very next paragraph rhetorical questions again sweep aside the argument. The author states that the projectors claim that there would result a gain of one day in seven, "which is now entirely lost, and consequently the Kingdom one Seventh the less considerable in Trade, Business, and Pleasure . . . ." The stately churches could also be used for "Theatres, Exchanges, Market-houses, common Dormitories, and other publick Edifices." Being incapable of seeing in church attendance any possible hindrance to business or pleasure, the baffled author merely floods his reader with a series of rhetorical questions and then, as before, drops the whole point and moves on to the next topic.

What if the Men of Pleasure are forced, one Day in the Week, to game at Home instead of the *Chocolate-House?* Are not the *Taverns* and *Coffee-Houses* open? Can there be  more convenient Season for taking a Dose of Physick? Are fewer Claps got upon *Sundays* than other Days? Is not that the chief Day for Traders to sum up the Accounts of the Week; and for Lawyers to prepare their Briefs? But I would fain know how it can be pretended, that the Churches are misapplied. Where are more Appointments and Rendezvouzes of Gallantry? Where more Care to appear in the foremost Box with greater Advantage of Dress? Where more Meetings for Business? Where more Bargains driven of all Sorts? And where so many Conveniences, or Incitements to Sleep?

The next argument of the projectors is treated in the same way: it is dismissed with a series of rhetorical questions, all of which tend to reduce the question to sheer nominalism. But, having done so, the author proceeds to argue the point at length even though he has already substantially nullified the point with rhetorical questions. The author states that the greatest advantage yet proposed for abolition is that parties and therefore all party strife would be "utterly extinguished." The author pauses wearily for a second to reflect that if this were certain, "I would submit, and be silent." But, he resumes,

will any Man say, that if the Words *Whoring, Drinking, Cheating, Lying, Stealing,* were, by Act of Parliament, ejected out of the *English* Tongue and Dictionaries; we should all awake next Morning chaste and temperate, honest and just, Lovers of Truth. Is this a fair Consequence? Or if the Physicians would forbid us to pronounce the Words *Pox, Gout, Rheumatism,* and *Stone;* would that Expedient serve like so many *Talismans* to destroy the Diseases themselves? Are Party and Faction rooted in Men's Hearts no deeper than Phrases borrowed from Religion; or founded upon no firmer principles? And is our Language so poor, that we cannot find other Terms to express them? Are Envy, Pride, Avarice and Ambition, such ill Nomenclators, that they cannot furnish Appellations for their Owners? Will not *Heydukes* and *Mamalukes,* and *Potshaws,* or any other Words formed at Pleasure, serve to distinguish those who are in the *Ministry* from others, who *would be in* it *if they could?* What, for Instance, is easier than to vary the Form of Speech; and instead of the Word *Church,* make it a Question in Politicks, Whether the Monument be in Danger? Because Religion was nearest at hand to furnish a few convenient Phrases; is our Invention so barren, we can find no others?

Having dropped these several questions into his reader's lap, the author argues by parallel example, pointing out that the parties which caused the civil war in Justinian's reign took their names quite illogically from the colors of the ribbons worn by racing horses.

The next argument is met with an argument, but the seventh argument (that prejudices of the old religion would be removed) is again parried, not this time with a rhetorical question, but merely with the counter assertion that the new education has already accomplished this end. Thus in six consecutive arguments there are five refusals to argue formally, and in three of these instances the author relies on the rhetorical question to nullify the projectors' position. Several purposes are served here. The author's refusing even to dignify the opposition's claims by treating them seriously as worthy of argument weakens the opposing position. The rhetorical questions just cited, although certainly they are apparently sincere within the ironic context, nevertheless are so couched that their tone is one of exasperation at having to answer such pointless proposals. Being at a loss as to how to answer such proposals, the author manages to imply that he is rather forced back onto the rhetorical question as the only means of comment. This tone is further underscored by the fact that in the first two uses of the device the author withholds all comment, thus emphasizing the ridiculous nature of the proposals; whereas, in treating the fifth proposal, the author pursues the proposal with an argument after having nullified it with a rhetorical question. Doing so softens the aspersion and implies a certain worth to the question which the other two lacked.

The rhetorical question is of course a kind of dormant argument, even though it is not a formal argument. The use of the rhetorical question also relaxes somewhat the otherwise incessant flow of the author's formal argument, thus giving a variety to the presentation. And, finally, this device helps Swift to control the emphasis of the essay as a whole. Assuming that the refusal to argue and the resort to the rhetorical question soften the hardness and the extreme clarity of a well-turned formal argument, one can observe that Swift has clustered this device in the anti-abolition section and has carefully kept it out of the more powerful pro-Christian section. In this latter section he follows in rapid-fire order four argued reasons for the retention of Christianity, thus concluding the main body of the essay on a more positive and firmer line of persuasion than the rhetorical question admits of. These, then, are the uses of the rhetorical questions in which the device is brought into full play as a substitute for formal argumentation. In addition to this major role is the lesser function that it performs within other arguments.

In paragraph twenty-one, the author turns to the projectors' claim that the abolition of Christianity will enlarge the basis of the Establishment and therefore lessen factionalism. He answers by arguing that the spirit of opposition is older than Christianity, that, for example, the "Opposition of Sectaries" is nowhere required in the Gospel: "Does the Gospel any where prescribe a starched squeezed Countenance, a stiff formal Gait, a Singularity of Manners and Habit, or any affected Modes of Speech, different from the reasonable Part of Mankind?" Yet, he continues, if Christianity were not present to absorb this kind of spleen, such humors must then be "spent in Contraventions to the Laws of the Land, and Disturbance of the Publick Peace." Here the rhetorical question has the simple task of implying the disaffected mien of the Puritan without the author's seeming himself to become a "sectary" in his attacking the Dissenters. Thus the device allows him to exculpate himself from the charge of factionalism which he is indirectly levelling against the dissenters. His subtle insertion of the one word *reasonable* gives the intended contrast and the intended answer to the question. The author concludes his answer to this question with a rhetorical question. Having expanded his argument that the spirit of opposition would operate in spite of the removal of Christianity and that therefore the Establishment could never be sufficiently broad to allow everyone entry, he concludes with the fine question "For what imports it, how large a Gate you open, if there will be always left a Number, who place a Pride and a Merit in refusing to enter?" This is the last sentence of the paragraph, which begins with the personification of the Spirit of Opposition. In this rhetorical question Swift returns to the specific subject of the opening sentence, identifies the dissenters as votaries of that goddess, and implies their irreligious position when he echoes and inverts the passage from the Sermon on the Mount: "Enter ye in at the strait gate: for wide is the gate, and broad is the way, that leadeth to destruction, and many there be which go in thereat: Because strait is the gate, and narrow is the way, which leadeth unto life, and few there be that find it." (St. Matthew, VII, 13-14.) The dissenters have on principle rejected the narrow gate and out of sheer perverseness also reject the broad gate.

In paragraph twenty-four the author urges the retention of Christianity so that the "strong Reasoners" and the men of "profound Learning" will have a subject matter which will properly display their great talents. Only this happy choice of subject matter has made these men prominent:

We are daily complaining of the great Decline of Wit among us; and would we take away the greatest, perhaps the only Topick we have left? Who would ever have suspected *Asgill* for a Wit, or *Toland* for a Philosopher, if the inexhaustible Stock of Christianity had not been at Hand to provide them with Materials? What other Subject through all Art or Nature could have produced Tindal for a profound Author, or furnished him with Readers? It is the wise Choice of the Subject that alone adorns and distinguishes the Writer.

The author uses a rhetorical question a final time in paragraph twenty-seven. In arguing that freedom of religion is freedom of thought and action, he asks, "For, of what use is Freedom of Thought, if it will not produce Freedom of Action; which is the sole End, how remote soever, in Appearance, of all Objections against Christianity?" This rhetorical question introduces the reasoning of the man who, through a long sorites, deduced that because a single error was found in one of the texts used for the proof of the Trinity, he could "safely whore and drink on, and defy the Parson." Through the rhetorical question Swift prepares for this passage by parodying in advance the logic of this man, a freethinker who has led himself to a position of atheism.

Thus Swift uses the rhetorical question in two distinctive and important ways: to vary the flow of formal argumentative forms, concentrating the rhetorical questions into the first section of the essay and omitting them from the stronger pro-Christian section; and, in the more standard classical usage, to express exasperation, to imply the obviousness of the point, and to make strong implications without simple, direct assertions.

### LESS FREQUENTLY USED DEVICES

The use of parenthesis in this essay is somewhat limited both in incidence and in function. In each of its four occurrences it functions only in the simple manner for which it is named; it in no way contributes peculiarly to the irony as it does in "A Modest Proposal."

In paragraph five the author states: "I hope, no Reader imagines me so weak to stand up in the Defence of *real* Christianity; such as used in primitive Times (if we may believe the Authors of those Ages) to have an Influence upon Mens Beliefs and Actions . . . ." Having previously reduced the "Gospel System" to just one of several systems now antiquated, he uses this parenthesis further to cast doubt upon that system which was so long ago abandoned. But even bothering to make clear that his defence is of nominal Christianity and certainly not of real Christianity has been only in the interest of complete clarity; only a few cavillers might have argued the point: "THEREFORE, I think this Caution was in itself altogether unnecessary, (which I have inserted only to prevent all possibility of cavilling) since every candid Reader will easily understand my Discourse to be intended only in Defence of *nominal* Christianity; the other having been for some Time wholly laid aside by general Consent, as utterly inconsistent with all our present Schemes of Wealth and Power." This parenthesis, plus the whole sentence in which it occurs, comes at a particularly important passage in the essay: Swift is here making the distinction between nominal and real Christianity the major axis for the ironic inversion of the essay. The most important single "fact" of the ironic inversion is inserted with great apology as a thing too obvious to need mention. But Swift, as if to remove all doubt of what his real statement is as opposed to his ironic norm of the essay, inserts this parenthesis in order to contrast the cavillers and the "candid Readers," correctly assuming that his readers will all fancy themselves among the "candid." Perhaps we might comment that the point is clear enough without this added warning of paragraph six and its parenthesis. However, in an essay as complex in argument and in point of view as this one, Swift might have felt that he could not be too clear.

"BUT why we should therefore cast off the Name and Title of Christians, although the general Opinion and Resolution be so violent for it; I confess I cannot (with Submission) apprehended the Consequence necessary." The little parenthesis is of course used here to help establish the author's tone of appropriate deference so necessary to the ethical proof.

In paragraph nine the parenthesis assumes a somewhat different function. After relating the incident of the two young gentlemen who, after having published a tract proving the nonexistence of God, were "by an unparallelled Severity, and upon I know not what *obsolete* Law, broke *only* for *Blasphemy,*" the author "rightly" fears the possibility of more persecution. Using one of the two proverbs in the essay, he comments, "And as it hath been wisely observed; if Persecution once begins, no Man alive knows how far it may reach, or where it will end." This is the last sentence of paragraph eight; paragraph nine begins with a new subject: Christianity is needed so that the wits will attack it instead of the government. This contention is "proved" by a second proverb, the statement of Tiberius *"Deorum offensa Diis curae."* To show the relation of this line of thought to the preceding section on persecution, Swift inserts the following parenthesis in order to give a verbal echo to paragraph eight:

As to the particular Fact related, I think it is not fair to argue from one Instance; perhaps another cannot be produced; yet (to the Comfort of all those, who may be apprehensive of Persecution) Blasphemy we know is freely spoke a Million of Times in every Coffee-House and Tavern, or wherever else *good Company* meet.

Then follows the second example of persecution for the minor offense of blasphemy (that of the breaking of the "English Free-born Officer"). The author's parenthesis is here not so much a rhetorical device of persuasion as it is a rhetorical device of composition, used to join two units of the same argument which has been interrupted.

The functions of the two proverbs are interesting. The Latin one serves as a proof for the argument that unless Christianity diverts such attacks, the wits will attack the government. Aristotle especially recommends argument from the proverb because it is a complete enthymeme which carries with it the ancient wisdom of the majority. The other use of a proverb (the first one, warning that no man knows where persecution might end) has little to do with the argument as such. It does, however, function importantly in non-argumentative persuasion, for it plays upon the fear and prejudice of the reader and prepares for the story of the breaking of the army officer, seventeen lines later.

However, there are much stronger appeals to the readers' passions and prejudices. These direct appeals fall into two areas: the readers' pride as an Englishman and his Protestant-English fear of the Roman Church. The first such appeal is the case of the English officer broken for blasphemy: "It must be allowed indeed, that to break an *English Free-born* Officer only for Blasphemy, was, to speak the gentlest of such an Action, a very high Strain of absolute Power." Emphasizing that the officer is *"Free-born"* and English draws forth the desired indignation. Also, *"Free-born"* seems to be a word play on "Free-thinker" and connects the diminution of "Free-thinker" to *"Free-born,"* calling to mind as it does the freethinker's nonconsequential argument that to be free-born gives a person the right (*license* is a better word) to think fallaciously. Swift has another and much more subtle use to make of the word *English* before he ends the paragraph. In the passage just quoted he has *"English Free-born"* to elicit the maximum pride of nationalism and patriotism, but with the phrase he has also set a trap for his English reader when the phrase *"English* Army" appears at the end of the paragraph:

Little can be said in excuse for the General [who broke the officer]; perhaps he was afraid it might give Offence to the Allies, among whom, for ought I know, it may be the Custom of the Country to believe a God. But if he argued, as some have done, upon a mistaken Principle, that an Officer who is guilty of speaking Blasphemy, may some time or other, proceed so far as to raise a Mutiny; the Consequence is, by no Means, to be admitted: For, surely the Commander of an *English* Army is like to be but ill obeyed, whose Soldiers fear and reverence him as little as they do a Deity.

The trap has been so set that either the English reader must accept the implication of gross impiety in an English army or he must see his English pride dashed to the ground. This deduction is of course based upon a reading of the sentence *as* irony. Within the ironic illusion there is no such trap.

The most elaborate (and the most humorous) of the appeals to national pride occurs in paragraph fifteen. This is the paragraph in which Swift reduces the whole argument of the essay to one of nominalism. His argument runs that Christianity just happened to be on the scene when party names were coined and that these names might just as easily have come from some other source. Surely, he says, English resourcefulness is great enough to find new names; surely the English language can yield new names; surely an Englishman's party principles are more deeply rooted than mere Christian nomenclature:

Are Party and Faction rooted in Mens hearts [i.e., not in their minds] no deeper than Phrases borrowed from Religion; or founded upon no firmer Principles? And is our Language so poor, that we cannot find other Terms to express them? Are Envy, Pride, Avarice and Ambition, such ill Nomenclators, that they cannot furnish Appellations for their Owners? . . . Because Religion was nearest at Hand to furnish a few convenient Phrases; is our Invention so barren, we can find no others?

The author appeals not only to English pride but also to English fears of the Roman Church. Swift has quite carefully prepared for this particular appeal to his reader's prejudice, and the steps are extremely interesting to follow. In paragraph twenty-one he makes the initial implication that the dissenters and the Romans have a great deal in common, but this notion is merely mentioned in passing. It is not mentioned again for several paragraphs, but then in paragraphs twenty-five and twenty-six the dissenter-Roman union is boldly made and used at the center of a major argument. Let us now examine these three paragraphs.

In paragraph twenty-one the main topic is the spirit of opposition. The author is arguing that the removal of Christianity would not remove party strife because "the Spirit of Opposition" is independent of Christianity. "Let us, for Instance, examine wherein the Opposition of Sectaries among us consists; we shall find Christianity to have no Share in it at all." Then he sketches the Dissenters in a mold at least as old as that of Jonson's Puritans at Bartholomew Fair: "Does the Gospel any where prescribe a starched squeezed Countenance, a stiff formal Gait, a Singularity of Manners and Habit, or any affected Modes of Speech, different from the reasonable Part of Mankind?" The government must provide some outlet for the "Enthusiasm" of such people. The Christian religion offers such a diversion: "If the Quiet of a State can be bought by only flinging Men a few Ceremonies to devour, it is a Purchase no wise Man would refuse. Let the Mastiffs amuse themselves about a Sheepskin stuffed with Hay, provided it will keep them from worrying the Flock." The Roman Church has solved this problem of enthusiasts by the institution of the several religious orders domiciled in convents: "The Institution of Convents abroad, seems in one Point a Strain of great Wisdom; there being few Irregularities in human Passions, that may not have recourse to vent themselves in some of those Orders; which are so many Retreats for the Speculative, the Melancholy, the Proud, the Silent, the Politick, and the Morose, to spend themselves, and evaporate the noxious Particles; for each of whom, we in this Island are forced to provide a several Sect of Religion, to keep them quiet. And whenever Christianity shall be abolished, the Legislature must find some other Expedient to employ and entertain them." The subtlety of the implication is delightful: the arch-despisers of the Roman way ought really to be in convents. The description of those who are in convents on the Continent is sufficiently similar to that of the dissenters, quoted above, for the deduction to be justified. Characteristically Swift drops this tentative, initial association of the two extremes and waits four paragraphs before he begins his major argument in which the Roman-dissenter connection becomes really important. This advance preparation is typical of Swift at his best.

In paragraphs twenty-five and twenty-six the argument runs as follows: the dissenters and the Romans have in common their desire to destroy the Establishment, and frequent historical example proves that the Roman Church has "at sundry Times" sent Roman Catholics to England to appear

"in the Guise of *Presbyterians, Anabaptists, Independents,*
and *Quakers,* according as any of these were most in Credit:
So, since the Fashion hath been taken up of exploding Religion, the *Popish* Missionaries have not been wanting to mix
with Free-Thinkers; among whom, *Toland,* the great Oracle
of the *Anti-Christians,* is an *Irish* Priest, the Son of an *Irish*
Priest; and the most learned and ingenious Author of a Book
called *The Rights of the Christian Church,* was, in a proper
Juncture, reconciled to the *Romish* Faith; whose true Son,
as appears by a Hundred Passages in his Treatise, he still continues." The Roman Catholics, after having joined with the
dissenters to overthrow the Establishment, would then with-
draw from the dissenters and establish their "Superstition":
". . . For, supposing Christianity to be extinguished, the
People will never be at Ease, till they find out some other
Method of Worship; which will as infallibly produce Superstition, as this will end in *Popery.*" The implication of this
statement is even more cutting in satire than the stated one:
Swift pretends to assume a complete separation between the
Roman Church and Christianity; indeed, the removal of
Christianity would, he says, merely hasten the advent of the
Roman Church in England. But he does not limit this observation to the Roman Church. Earlier (in paragraph 25) he
makes a similar assumption as the basis for a comment about
the Establishment, when he states that the removal of Christianity might tend to endanger the Establishment: ". . . I am
far from presuming to affirm or think, that the Church is in
Danger at present, or as Things now stand; but we know
not how soon it may be so, when the Christian Religion is
repealed." Such bungling assumptions further indicate Swift's
author's confused notions of Christianity and the Church and
point up the nominalism of the whole argument. This aspect
of the passage under discussion is a good example of one of
the rhetorical means through which Swift imbues his essay
with an illusion of tightness of argument and of overwhelming
"rightness": the same assumptions and assertions keep weaving in and out of the paragraphs. In one paragraph they remain unstated, prior assumptions, only to reappear elsewhere
at the center of major arguments. Such a technique is not so
much fugue-like as it is spatial; the ideas seem to move in a

third dimension, pausing in the background and then moving brilliantly to the reader's focus in the foreground, then dipping back again. It is amazing to note the small number of really *different* ideas which the essay contains; it is the iteration of them that helps lend them strength.

The device of verbal irony is scarcely employed within this ironical essay, there being only two instances, each of which is simple understatement. The author states that the objection against paying a "Sett of Men" to "bawl" from a pulpit every seventh day "is, I think, a little unworthy so refined an Age as ours." Referring to the anti-Establishmentarianism views of several groups of freethinkers, the author says that nothing could be more notorious than that they "are Persons of little Zeal for the present Ecclesiastical Establishment." These simple understatements reflect the urbane wit of the author and, as such, contribute through their tone to the character of the writer and, in turn, to the ethical proof.

There is present, however, another kind of irony which operates in conjunction with anticlimax. Loosely speaking, of course, one might say that all irony of inversion is anticlimactic in so far as the concluding remark is an unexpected reversal. For example, in the final paragraph of the present essay, the author states that the abolishing of Christianity might possibly cause the stock of the Bank and the East-India Company to fall "at least One *per Cent.* And, since that is Fifty Times more than ever the Wisdom of our Age thought fit to venture for the *Preservation* of Christianity, there is no Reason we should be at so great a Loss, meerly for the Sake of *destroying* it." This ironic and startling concluding clause is basically anticlimactic to the extent that, whatever direction the sentence might have built toward, Swift has chosen rather to undercut it with a fine ironic reversal. Obviously this technique is central to the irony of the whole essay, and its general movement (the rising idea and the rising cadence ascending only to be cut down) can be seen over and over in the essay. This is a generalized anticlimax operating with the irony and is not the particular use of specific classical anticlimax.

Indeed, there are only two instances of anticlimax which

tend to be specific enough to be called anticlimax instead of irony, and the first of these is debatable. Both occur in paragraph nine. Near the end of that paragraph the author vigorously complains about the English officer who was broken merely for blasphemy. It can't be argued, he says, that such an officer might someday lead a mutiny, for who would follow him? "For, surely the Commander of an *English* Army is like to be but ill obeyed, whose Soldiers fear and reverence him as little as they do a Deity." This, one might notice, might just as well be termed pure irony of inversion as anticlimax.

The one good example of anticlimax is in the conclusion of the following sentence:

Great Wits love to be free with the highest Objects; and if they cannot be allowed a *God* to revile or renounce; they will *speak Evil of Dignities*, abuse the Government, and reflect upon the Ministry; which I am sure, few will deny to be a much more pernicious Consequence; according to the saying of *Tiberius; Deorum offensa Diis curae.*

This sentence partakes of ironical inversion even as the anticlimax is operating in the nouns *dignities, government,* and *ministry.* The whole series is placed in ironical opposition to God and the highest objects. As if feeling that the anticlimax did not stand out boldly enough, Swift has added the clue "which I am sure few will deny to be of much more pernicious Consequence." With the exception of this one example, then, the device of anticlimax operates as a general principle of irony rather than as a particularized functioning of the smaller device of rhetorical anticlimax.

Personification is used only once in the essay, and its very uniqueness adds to its force. In paragraph twenty-one the author turns to the anti-Christian argument that the removal of Christianity will remove parties and factional strife, to which he replies that "there is one darling Inclination of Mankind, which usually affects to be a Retainer to Religion, although she be neither its Parent, its God-mother, nor its Friend; I mean the Spirit of Opposition, that lived long before Christianity, and can easily subsist without it." When, in an essay otherwise devoid of personification, this vigorous Lady Opposition springs to life, the idea takes on a vividness not likely to be gained by a less forceful method. Classical rhetoricians expanded this device into a full genealogy of the personified idea; other writers of Swift's generation made the same use of genealogical personification (most notable, perhaps, is that in *The Dunciad*). In other essays Swift too has elaborated fully such genealogies;[8] however, here he merely hints at the ancient lineage of the Spirit of Opposition through the words *Parent* and *God-mother*. Her being much older than Christianity hints vaguely that she might be related to ancient gods and goddesses and that these sectaries merely by being partisans pay her due homage.

This personification goes beyond simple personification, for, happily, the Spirit of Opposition is emblematic of a major argument in the essay as well as of the whole political point of view of the essay and of Swift and his associates. In this essay and throughout the *Examiner* papers Swift decries factionalism, which he and his group virtually equated with party. The concept of ministerial, party administration of the government was just beginning to evolve during the reign of Queen Anne; Harley and St. John struggled with the Whigs and with each other as much from personal motives as from motives of party and principle. It was the role of the next minister, Walpole, to establish the working arrangement of ministerial government. Indeed many historians of the period call him England's first Prime Minister. In the pre-ministerial days of Anne's reign, the horror of factional party lines can better be appreciated. Possibly because Swift and his colleagues were so continually plagued with the spectre of this "one darling Inclination of Mankind," she springs into such vivid relief in this essay. At any rate, the functioning of the device is twofold: it gives unusual strength to the expression of the idea, and it serves as a kind of emblem of a major argument within and behind the essay.

### CONCLUSIONS

Non-argumentative devices of rhetoric do not operate in such an all-consuming manner in this essay as they do in "A Modest Proposal." However, in the considerable degree to which they do function in this essay, they are as fundamental to the irony of the essay as they are to the irony in "A Modest Proposal."

The ethical proof informs every paragraph of the essay: the author's patriotism, fairness, reasonableness, competence, and argumentative courage are humanly tempered by occasional muddle-headedness. The ethical proof establishes the character of the author and thus fundamentally sets up the pose upon which all of the ironic structure must rest. The double-edged diminution reduces both sides of the argument to the level of nominalism so that Swift can with the substitution of a single word accomplish his strongest ironic stroke. While this is happening, the amplification of the freethinkers is partially counterbalancing the diminution of their position. More importantly, the vocabulary involved in the amplification quietly but unceasingly establishes the satiric norm of the essay, imputing the inverted value-system to the whole society. With only slightly less frequency the appeal to a generalized authority is accomplishing the same end. Mingled with the almost constant flow of formal arguments is the well-placed rhetorical question which serves to vary the pattern of argument and to imply that some of the arguments for the abolition are simply too insignificant to deserve formal rebuttal. With telling force the author appeals to his readers' pride as Englishmen and to their prejudices and fears of the Roman Church, and with a masterful sleight-of-hand he is through this appeal able to lump together both extremes of the opposition to the Establishment so deftly that the dissenters and Romans hardly suspected that they had a common bed. Added to these uses of the devices fundamental to the essay are the several other devices which, although they do not contribute peculiarly to the creation of the irony, do lend their added weight of tradition of style and method.

## Chapter IV

# "A Vindication
# of Lord Carteret"

John Carteret, Earl Granville, served as Lord-Lieutenant of Ireland from 1724 to 1730. Not only was he the most sincere Vice-Roy which Ireland had during the eighteenth century, but also, having been a pupil of Stanhope, he was one of the finest statesmen of the century. Descended from two great families—the Carterets and the Granvilles, both of whom had been in England since the Conquest—, he came into his title at the age of five, and by the age of twenty-nine, an age when, Swift remarks, most young men are leading dissipated lives in the chocolate houses, he had accomplished a brilliant mission to the court of Sweden, where he negotiated a series of intricate treaties of peace among Sweden, Prussia, Denmark, and Hanover. Slow communications somewhat isolating him in the north, it was his boldness and his ability to make good decisions quickly and independently which enabled him to succeed in this mission.

In the ministry of Walpole, Carteret was made Secretary of State for the Department of the South (even though it was the languages and politics of northern Europe in which he was unusually well grounded). Because he had less success at the French court, Walpole and Newcastle seized their first opportunity to "deport" him to Ireland, for he was far too powerful an orator to remove from the ministry but leave free to speak in the House of Lords. Carteret was one of the few Lord-Lieutenants actually to live in Ireland most of the year and to turn his efforts seriously to the amelioration of ills in Ireland. Although he was powerless to accomplish any major needed reforms of the whole system of English government of Ireland, nevertheless he perceived these ills and did what he could, which was a great deal more than any other

Lord-Lieutenant had done. One such effort is revealed by his attempts to appoint Irishmen to more posts in their own government, which act forms one of the main topics in Swift's essay. Walpole so disapproved of this policy that when in 1727 upon the accession of King George II Carteret was issued a new commission, he was specifically barred from the power of nominating deans, members of the Board of Exchequer, officers of the army, or governors of forts, without the express permission of the Secretary of State.

Carteret was a well-educated man, having attended Westminster School and Christ Church, Oxford; he had a ready wit and a wide range of interests. He and Swift had been good friends since 1710, and nothing jarred this friendship, not even the commotion over Wood's halfpence, during which they found themselves on opposite sides of the struggle publicly.[1] In fact Swift's vindication is a defence of Carteret's preference for having men like Swift about him. He used Swift as a measurement of his good governing, for upon his return to England in 1730 he was asked how he ruled Ireland. His answer was "I pleased Dean Swift." In a letter to Gay, Swift characterized Carteret's administration of Ireland in these terms: "I believe my Lord Carteret, since he is no longer Lieutenant, may not wish me ill, and I have told him often that I only hated him as Lieutenant, I confess he had a genteeler manner of binding the chains of this kingdom, than most of his predecessors. . . ."[2] It was his good administration of a basically bad system which made Swift only half humorously cry out, "What the vengeance brought you among us? Get you back, get you back; pray God Almighty send us our boobies again!"

## THE ETHICAL PROOF

Because this essay is fundamentally one of ironical praise and because Swift was not interested in writing a bitterly lacerating essay about his good friend Lord Carteret, the rhetorical problem faced by Swift was to employ a device which would damn gently rather than harshly through strong ironic contrast stemming from extreme over-praise of the wrong qualities and extreme anger at Carteret's real virtues.[3] To accomplish this result, Swift relies upon several aspects of the ethical proof: he creates a moderate Whig who concedes the truth of Carteret's various "faults" but who can reasonably argue that in spite of these concessions, Carteret can be extenuated of the charges of disaffection to the ministry and the Whig party. Concession is the informing device of the essay; and, while concession is operating powerfully at the strictly argumentative level of the rhetoric, it is operating just as successfully in establishing the ethical proof. Nineteen paragraphs are given over in whole or in part to this double-functioning concession (its use as the main line of argument and its use in establishing the reasonableness of the author).

Coupled with the reasonableness of the author is the abundant evidence of the good and loyal Whiggism of the author. Swift has his author reveal this good Whiggism through overt statements, through the stance which the author assumes (that a moderate Whig has the good of the kingdom more at heart than the zealot Whig), and through associating with the Whig author and Whigs in general the qualities of a modern. This last named part of the ethical proof allows the author to criticize Lord Carteret's scholarship simply from a point of ignorance instead of one of anger over Carteret's good qualities as scholar and gentleman. For the "vindication" to be "successful" politically, it must be written by a man of Carteret's own party who, not blind to his "faults," can still prove Carteret's loyalty to his party. The general movement of the essay further elucidates these characterizing remarks: the author concedes the fact that Cartert has the "faults" of good scholarship, sound wit, good breeding, classical tastes, and impeccable personal conduct. He further concedes that the Lord-Lieutenant has favoured with public or church office four persons alleged not to be loyal Whigs. Drawing up Whig and Tory "accounts," however, he finds that the Whigs have profited £27,404 and the Tories (or alleged Tories) £111. He concludes that "the Ballance, I conceive, *seems to lie*" on the Whigs' advantage.

Swift's "author" is a moderate Whig who displays his reasonableness, his "modernity," his strong argumentative position, his concession, his thoroughness, his willingness to discuss every case brought against Lord Carteret—no matter how damaging—, his occasional muddle-headedness (one wonders what his exact opinion of Hobbes and the curators of Bedlam is), and his occasional justifiable wrath.

The opening paragraph of the essay starts the ethical proof, indicating as it does the fairness of the author and his sincere desire to get at the truth and the initial concession that some reasonable questions against Lord Carteret can be raised:

IN order to treat this important Subject, with the greatest Fairness and Impartiality; perhaps it may be convenient to give some Account of his *Excellency*; in whose Life and Character, there are certain Particulars, which might give a very just Suspicion of some Truth in the Accusation he lies under.

The author states that Lord Carteret attended Oxford, but must concede that "with a Singularity, scarce to be justified" Carteret learned more of the classical languages and philosophy "than properly became a Person of his Rank; indeed much more of each than most of those who are forced to Live by their Learning, will be at the unnecessary Pains to load their Heads with." And this is "the Rock he split on, upon his first Appearance in the World"; the influence of the Court could never "wipe off the Stain, nor wash out the Tincture of his University Acquirements and Disposition."

The author must concede yet more:

To this, another Misfortune was added; that it pleased God to endow him with great natural Talents, Memory, Judgment, Comprehension, Eloquence, and Wit: And, to finish the Work, all these were fortified, even in his Youth, with the Advantages received by such Employments, as are best fitted both to exercise and polish the Gifts of Nature and Education; having been Ambassador in several Courts, when his Age would hardly allow him to take a Degree; and made principal Secretary of State, at a Period when, according to Custom, he ought to have been busied in losing his Money at a Chocolate-House; or in other Amusements equally laudable and epidemick among Persons of Honour.

There is one rather serious indiscretion of Carteret which the author must admit. It "can be proved upon" his Excellency that he reads books in Latin and Greek daily and that they might be found in his dressing room "if it were carefully searched." And "there is Reason to suspect, that some of the said Books have been privately conveyed to him by *Tory* Hands." Further, he has been known to read such books during Sessions, "to the great Neglect of publick Affairs." "I OWN," admits the author, "there may be some Grounds for this Charge; because I have it from good Hands, that when His Excellency is at Dinner, with one or two Scholars at his Elbows, he grows a most unsupportable, and unintelligible Companion to all the fine Gentlemen round the Table."

In paragraph eight, the author concedes yet another point: "I CANNOT deny that His Excellency lies under another great Disadvantage." Even though Carteret is a handsome youth of great spirit and vigor, he has been so dull as to lead "in a most unexemplary Manner . . . a regular domestick Life; [and he] discovers a great Esteem, and Friendship, and Love for his Lady, as well as a true Affection for his Children. . . ." And when he has friends in to dine, he does not "enough reflect, whether the Person may possibly in former Days, have lain under the Imputation of a *Tory;* nor, at such Times, do the natural or *affected* Fears of *Popery* and the *Pretender,* make any Part of the Conversation; I presume, because neither *Homer, Plato, Aristotle,* nor *Cicero,* have made any mention of them."

These are the principal concessions which the author finds himself obligated, for fairness' sake, to admit in the character of Lord Carteret: "THESE I freely acknowledge to be his Excellency's Failings: Yet, I think it is agreed by Philosophers and Divines; that some Allowance ought to be given to human Infirmity, and to the Prejudices of a wrong Education."

Some evidence of the author's good Whig principles has already been cited in connection with reasonableness as a component of the ethical proof. Other examples occur in the process of diminution, which will be considered subsequently. At the present those indicants of this phase of the ethical proof not covered in the other two areas will be dealt with. Establishing the author as a good Whig is essential to the persuasive power of the essay because the essay is by a Whig "author," for a Whig, and against Whigs who are more extreme than the two former.

The author gives in the second paragraph the first indication beyond the title itself that he is a good Whig and a loyal subject even though he is outspoken in his old loyalty to Charles I:

HE [Carteret] is descended from two noble, antient, and most loyal Families, the *Carterets*, and the *Granvilles*: Too much distinguished, I confess, for what they acted, and what they suffered in defending the former Constitution in Church and State, under King *Charles* the Martyr; I mean that every Prince on Account of whose Martyrdom, *a Form of Prayer, with Fasting, was enjoined by Act of Parliament, to be used on the 30th Day of* January *every* Year, *to implore the Mercies of God, that the Guilt of that sacred and innocent Blood, might not be visited on us or our Posterity*; as we may read at large in our *Common-Prayer Books*. Which Day hath been solemnly kept, even within the Memory of many Men now alive.

In paragraph thirteen the author seems to include himself when he asks of the Whig zealots that Whigs "of the *old fashioned Stamp*," who are not so involved in immediate party matters and who therefore have more time for more detached judgment and writing, should be granted freedom to print their thoughts for the kingdom without being immediately branded as traitors: "Now I can, by no Means, approve our usual Custom of cursing and railing at this Species of Thinkers, under the Names of *Tories, Jacobites, Papists, Libellers, Rebels*, and the like."

In arguing that the chief governor of the kingdom should be allowed to choose his own companions without regard to the strictness of their conformity to the party line, the author states both his position and Carteret's: Does it matter whether these companions in former times have been "suspected for differing from the *Orthodox* in some speculative Opinions of Persons and Things, which cannot affect the fundamental Principles of a sound Whig"?

In considering Dr. Delany's party loyalty, the author finally concludes that since Delany can be proved to be neither Whig nor Tory, he shall be considered "ONE OF US: But, like a new *Free-Mason*, who hath not yet learned all the Dialect of the Mystery." The author is able subtly to imply that policies really good for the kingdom are not peculiarly party principles in the first place, as he says, "Neither can he justly be accused of any *Tory* Doctrines; except, perhaps, some among those few, with which that *wicked Party* was charged, during the Heighth of Power; but have been since transferred for the most *solid Reasons,* to the *whole Body* of our firmest Friends."

Turning himself even more specifically to the creation of the ethical proof, Swift inserts an extremely long classical digression, which runs from paragraph ten to paragraph twenty-six. The purpose of this digression is two-fold: it justifies the Whig author against the extreme element of his own party, the "Patriots," and it further extenuates Lord Carteret by indicating other areas of Dublin life in which party label is not always so nicely investigated as it is by the patriots with reference to the Lord-Lieutenant's companions and appointments.

The author opens the digression by conceding that he realizes that he is more moderate than some Whigs: "I AM well aware, how much my Sentiments differ from the orthodox Opinion of one or two principal Patriots, (at the Head of whom I name with Honour *Pistorides*).[4] For these have decided the Matter directly against me, by declaring, that no Person who was ever known to lie under the Suspicion of one single *Tory* Principle; or who had been once seen at a great Man's Levee in the *Worst of Times,*[5] should be allowed to come within the Verge of the Castle. . . ." However, "I dare assert, that this Maxim hath been often controlled [i.e., limited in application]; and that on the contrary, a considerable Number of *early Penitents* have been received into Grace, who are now an *Ornament, Happiness,* and *Support* to the Nation."

The author further points out that he hears no "murmuring" on other points in which this maxim is controlled. Only one instance, he says, need be cited. "I have not heard that any Care hath hitherto been taken, to discover whether Madam *Violante*[6] be a *Whig* or *Tory* in her Principles . . . I am told that she openly professeth herself to be a HIGH-FLYER; and it is not improbable, by her *Outlandish* Name she may also be a *Papist* in her Heart." Nevertheless, persons of quality in both parties openly caress this "dangerous Female" and contribute handsomely to her support, "without the least Apprehensions from a *Grand-Jury*; or even from 'Squire

*Hartly Hutcheson*[7] himself, that *zealous Prosecutor of Hawkers and Libels.*"

The author makes a digression from his digression in order to insert a noble plea that writers like Dean Swift be allowed to speak:

I CONFESS, there is one Evil which I could wish our Friends would think proper to redress. There are many *Whigs* in this Kingdom of the *old fashioned Stamp*, of whom we might make very good Use; they bear the same Loyalty with us, to the *Hanoverian* Family, in the Person of King *George* the IId. The same Abhorrence of the *Pretender*, with the Consequents of *Popery* and *Slavery*; and the same Indulgence to *tender Consciences*: But having nothing to ask for themselves, and therefore the more Leisure to think for the Publick; they are often apt to entertain Fears, and melancholly Prospects, concerning the State of their Country, the Decay of Trade, the Want of Money, the miserable Condition of the People, with other Topicks of like Nature; all which do equally concern both *Whig* and *Tory*; who, if they have any Thing to lose, must be equally Sufferers. Perhaps one or two of these melancholly Gentlemen, will sometimes venture to publish their Thoughts in Print: Now I can, by no Means, approve our usual Custom of cursing and railing at this Species of Thinkers, under the names of *Tories, Jacobites, Papists, Libellers, Rebels,* and the like.

Making a rapid ironic shift, Swift weeps crocodile tears for that "poor, angry, bustling, well-meaning Mortal *Pistorides*" who has been so libelled and whom "one single Wag" has pelted, pestered, and pounded and who has "promised never to forsake him, living or dead." This "one single Wag" is Swift. Continuing the subject, Swift characterizes himself as a wit in the following terms: "OF the like Spirit, too often, is that implacable Race of Wits; against whom there is no Defence but Innocence, and Philosophy; Neither of which is likely to be at Hand. . . ."

The author continues his digression against the extreme Whigs by expressing his pity also that "that other miserable Creature *Traulus*;[8] who although of somewhat a different Species, yet seems very far to outdo even the Genius of *Pistorides*, in that miscarrying Talent of railing without Consistency or Discretion, against the most innocent Persons,

according to the present Scituation of his Gall and Spleen."
A person, the author continues, who attacks a man in the
vilest manner and simultaneously embraces him as friend
publicly, whispering to him that "it was *all for his Service*,"
lays himself open to an attack by a certain "political *Surgeon*,"
who is, of course, Swift himself:

> This proceeding, I am bold to think a great Failure in Prudence;
> and I am afraid lest such a Practitioner, with a Body so *open*,
> so *foul*, and so *full of Sores*, may fall under the Resentment of
> an incensed political *Surgeon*, who is not in much Renown for
> his Mercy upon great Provocation: Who, without waiting for
> his Death, will *flay*, and *dissect* him alive; and to the View of
> Mankind, lay open all the disordered Cells of his Brain, the
> Venom of his Tongue, the Corruption of his Heart, and Spots
> and Flatuses of his Spleen—And all this for *Three-Pence*.

Finally, in paragraph twenty, Swift makes the identification
of this political surgeon as the Whig of the "*old fashioned
Stamp*" mentioned in paragraph thirteen:

> I APPREHEND that if all this should be set out to the World
> by an angry Whig of the *old* Stamp; the unavoidable Con-
> sequence must be a Confinement of our *Friend* for some Months
> *more* to his Garret; and thereby depriving the Publick for so
> long a Time, and in so *important a Juncture*, of his useful Talents
> in their Service. . . .

The author rejects any palliation for Traulus. Some excuse
him because of his madness; the author will not because the
authorities at Bedlam have assured him that madness merely
frees a man to show to its fullest his natural character and
Traulus in madness merely proves his vileness. The author
concedes that some people excuse Traulus on the grounds
of his astounding wit and oratorical ability to argue on both
sides eloquently, but the author cannot excuse a man who
loves a jest better than a friend and who "to gain the Reputation of the first *Orator* of the Kingdom" would not "scruple
to lose all the *Friends* he had in the World."

After asserting (and thereby demonstrating once again his
fairness) that "I HAVE placed this Reasoning in the strongest
Light, that I think it will bear; and have nothing to answer,
but that allowing it as much Weight as the Reader shall please,

it hath constantly met with ill success in the Mouth of our *Friend*; but whether for Want of good Luck, or good Management, I suspend my Judgment," the author concludes his digression, being careful to indicate its relevance to the whole essay:

> TO return from this long Digression; if Persons in high Stations have been allowed to chuse *Wenches*, without Regard even to Difference in Religion, yet never incurred the least Reflection on their Loyalty, or their Protestantism; shall the Chief Governor of a great Kingdom be censured for chusing a *Companion*, who may formerly have been suspected for differing from the *Orthodox* in some speculative Opinions of Persons and Things, which cannot affect the fundamental Principles of a sound *Whig?*

With this statement the author thus draws his digression to a close, identifies it by classical *genre*, and indicates that it was made to show the general milieu in which Lord Carteret is being so harshly and unfairly judged. This is the rhetorical purpose to which the author admits. Of course, it can also be seen that Swift uses the digression further to develop the ethical proof by indicating the distinction between the moderate Whig author and the extreme Whig patriots.

The author continues his concessions. What recourse for good conversation has a governor of Ireland, "whose unfortunate weak Side it happens to be for the several Reasons abovementioned, that he hath encouraged the Attendance of *one* or *two* Gentlemen distinguished for their Taste, Wit, and their Learning," when the zeal of men of his own party has "*eaten up* their *Understandings*"? The time of these men is utterly taken up with schemes for advancement in this world; and, although they are valuable to a governor, they make "the most disagreeable Companions to all who have that unfortunate Turn of Mind peculiar to his Excellency, and perhaps to five or six more in a Nation." The author does "not deny it possible" that "a Favourer of the Times" might have been born with those "useless Talents, which, in former Ages, qualifyed a Man to be a Poet, or a Philosopher. All I contend for, is that where the true Genius of Party once enters, it *sweeps the House clean*, and leaves room for many *other Spirits* to take joint Possession, until the *last State of that Man is exceedingly* better *than the first*."

In paragraph thirty the author alludes again to his concession that Carteret's education is most unfortunate, as is also his poor taste to read Greek at Sessions and to chat at table with scholars. The next paragraph pushes his concession even further:

I WILL venture one Step further; which is, freely to confess, that this mistaken Method of educating Youth in the Knowledge of antient Learning and Language, is too apt to spoil their *Politicks* and *Principles*; because the Doctrine and Examples of the Books they read, teach them Lessons *directly contrary in every Point*, to the *present Practice* of the World. . . .

Indeed, "Hobbes most judiciously observes, that the Writings of the *Greeks* and *Romans*, made young Men imbibe" a distaste for absolutism in princes and first ministers and to esteem liberty and property.

The author follows with another concession, but this time he quickly extenuates it by showing historical parallels: "I COULD heartily wish his Excellency would be more condescending to the *Genius* of the Kingdom he governs; to the Condition of the Times, and to the Nature of the Station he fills." Yet it is recorded that "Agesilaus" was caught riding a hobby-horse with his children and Socrates dancing by himself at fourscore; that Caesar Augustus used to play with boys, some of whom *might* have been "Sons of *Tories*"; that "*Scipio* and *Lelius*, (I forget their *Christian* Names, and whether they were Poets or Generals,) often played at *Duck* and *Drake*, with smooth Stones on a River." In the parenthesis the author quite generously admits his ignorance, and he later concedes that he has these stories only from a story book. But if they be true, ". . . I cannot imagine why our most zealous Patriots may not a little indulge his Excellency, in an Infirmity which is not morally Evil" and which gives no public scandal by allowing him twice a week to converse with particular persons, after public business has been attended to. They can do no harm in conning over "their old *exploded* Readings," even though these particular friends "may not have made so publick a Declaration of their political Faith in all its Parts, as the Business of the Nation requires. . . ."

The boldest way in which the author indicates his earnest desire to get at the truth of the charges against Lord Carteret is his turning directly to a detailed discussion of the most prominent cases complained of by the patriots: "BUT, in order to clear his Excellency more fully from this Accusation of shewing his Favours to *High-flyers*, *Tories*, and *Jacobites*; it will be necessary to come to Particulars." The author, fearless in his position of right, does not hesitate to name and discuss the four appointments which the detractors of Carteret believe to be their strongest proof against the Lord-Lieutenant, the awarding of livings to Dr. Sheridan, Mr. Stopford, and Dr. Delany, and the awarding of a grant to supply a barrack for the King's troop on the property of Sir Arthur Acheson.

The first appointment of a person with Tory connections was that of Dr. Thomas Sheridan to a church-living of almost one hundred pounds; Dr. Sheridan was also made one of the Lord-Lieutenant's chaplains. But this appointment "happened so early in his Excellency's Government, as it may be justly supposed he had not been informed of that Gentleman's Character, upon so *dangerous* an Article." The worth of Dr. Sheridan was brought to Carteret's attention when Sheridan's students presented a tragedy in Greek and invited Carteret. The play was written in an "*unknown* language" by "some Heathen Author; but whether it contained any *Tory* or *High-Church* Principles, must be left to the Consciences of the *Boys*, the *Doctor*, and his *Excellency*: The *only* Witnesses in this Case, whose Testimonies can be depended upon."

Being impressed by the Doctor's sound classical scholarship and the sound training of his students, Lord Carteret soon gave him a living and a place on the roll of chaplains, but not before he had received "strong Recommendations from Persons of undoubted Principles, *fitted to the Times*; who thought themselves bound in Justice, Honour, and Gratitude, to do the Doctor a good Office, in return for the Care he had taken of their Children, or those of their Friends." But a terrible "Catastrophe" befell Dr. Sheridan. Swift has his author tell this amusing and true story: it happened by complete chance that the absent-minded Dr. Sheridan was invited to preach at Cork on his way down to his new parish; the day happened to be August 1, the day for the annual commemoration of the ascension of the House of Hanover to the British throne. Pulling out one of his few old sermons, Dr. Sheridan, in perfect innocence, preached upon the text "Sufficient unto the day is the evil thereof." It further happened that Lord Allen, a "Man *of no large Dimensions of Boby or Mind*," was in the congregation and immediately sounded the alarm of this alleged disaffection against the House of Hanover. The author observes that the clamor raised was so great that "we in *Dublin* could apprehend no less than an Invasion by the *Pretender*, who must be landed in the *South*. The Result was, that the Doctor must be struck out of the Chaplains List, and appear no more at the Castle; yet whether he were then, or be to this Day, a *Whig* or a *Tory*, I think is a Secret. . . ." The author further relates that his friends had frequently heard Sheridan preach this sermon and that it made no reference to the government, a pary, or (for that matter) "the Subject of the Day." The author justly concludes that

In this Incident there seems to have been an Union of Events, that will probably never happen again to the End of the World; or, at least, like the grand Conjunction in the Heavens; which, I think, they say can arrive but once in Twenty Thousand Years.

The second appointee the author treats of is Mr. James Stopford, whom Carteret made Vicar of Finglass at a salary of about one hundred pounds per year. He is the second "if I am right in my Chronology": the author is ready to admit his fallibility in such details. Since Mr. Stopford is of such a scholarly bent as to be totally uninterested in all matters of party ("which I allow to be a great Omission"), the author finds that Lord Carteret did no great wrong in appointing such a political non-entity.

Dr. Patrick Delany, the third appointee of questioned party loyalty, lay under the disadvantage of having received a good University of Dublin appointment at the hands of Sir Constantine Phipps, Lord Chancellor of Ireland appointed by Queen Anne, her of "the worst of times." Dr. Delany was recommended to the Lord-Lieutenant by several persons, including the late Archbishop of Dublin and Dean Swift.

Carteret liked Delany because of the latter's "fatal Turn of Mind towards *Heathenish* and *outlandish* Books and Languages." When Delany was virtually forced out of his academic living by the "Managers" of the University "(which it may not be for their Honour to mention)", Carteret gave Delany two livings, which, added to the third which he already possessed from the University, brought him about £300 annually; he had earlier resigned a combined income from the University of about three times this amount. But Dr. Delany's political opinions have never been known:

BUT since the Doctor hath not, in any of his Writings, his Sermons, his Actions, his Discourse, or his Company, discovered one single Principle of either *Whig* or *Tory*; and that the Lord Lieutenant still continues to admit him; I shall boldly pronounce him ONE OF US: But like a new *Free-Mason*, who hath not yet learned all the Dialect of the Mystery.

At this point the author gives a tentative evaluation of his proof, generously allowing that of the three, only Dr. Sheridan cannot easily be cleared of all suspicion:

I HAVE now done with the Clergy: And upon the strictest Examination have not been able to find above one of that Order, against whom any *Party* Suspicion can lye; which is the unfortunate Gentleman, Doctor *Sheridan*, who by mere Chance-medley shot his own Fortune dead with a single *Text*.

The fourth and last case urged against Carteret is his having awarded a contract to Sir Arthur Acheson, the only layman "of the *Tory* Stamp, who since the beginning of his Excellency's Government, did ever receive any Mark of his Favour." He is "reported to be an acknowledged *Tory*; and, what is almost as bad, a *Scholar* into the Bargain." It is rumored that this gentleman is to have a grant to furnish a barrack for the King's soldiers, at a rent of £60 per year. In return he is to expend £500 to put the building and grounds into proper order. The author calculates that Sir Arthur will be liable to the following losses annually: £30 in interest had he invested the £500; £5 in poultry which the troopers will catch; £8 in sheep which the troopers will destroy; £6 in game for an area of five miles around. This total loss is £49, which, subtracted from the £60 rent paid by the Crown, will leave Sir Arthur a net gain of £11 annually.

It is true that there is one collateral advantage for Sir Arthur's whole neighbourhood: the "Breed of Mankind, and particularly that of *good Protestants*" will be greatly multiplied by the troopers, and this will "fully compensate the Loss of Cattle and Poultry." But the author is quick to admit his inability to calculate this gain: "But I am not so skilful in Arithmetick, as to compute the Value." The author further points out his moderation in the conservative nature of his base figures and calculations:

I HAVE reckoned one *per Cent.* below the Legal Interest for the Money that Sir *Arthur* must expend: And Valued the Damage in the other Articles very moderately. However, I am confident he may with good Management be a *Saver* at least; which is a *prodigious Instance of Moderation* in our Friends towards a professed *Tory*, whatever Merit he may pretend by the Unwillingness he hath shewn to make his Excellency uneasy in his Administration."

The author now addresses himself to his general conclusion to the whole essay, and again he avails himself of mathematical proof, first pausing to point out that the cases under discussion have after all been concerned with persons only allegedly or superficially *Tory* in principles of party and that it is

but too remarkable, that, in a neighbouring Nation (where this dangerous Denomination of Men is incomparably more Numerous, more Powerful, and of consequence more Formidable) *real Tories* can often with much less Difficulty, obtain very high Favours from the Government, than their *reputed* Brethren can arrive to the lowest in ours. I observe this with all possible Submission to the Wisdom of their Policy; which, however, will not, I believe, dispute the Praise of Vigilance with ours."

Rhetorically this is a strong counterbalance to the many pages of concessions which the author has generously and reasonably granted. The whole movement has been concession, and here at the end of the essay Swift must in five rather brief paragraphs place a weight so heavy as to tip the scales in the opposite direction. This task is partially accomplished in this single implied argument of the situation in Scotland and in England, for doing so allows him to brand the whole accusation to be a tempest in a teapot, since no "*real Tories*" are involved, as they are in England, where they are strong enough to make their demands sufficiently forceful to get results. The author relies mainly, however, upon his mathematical proof: the net profit of the alleged Tories is £111 (£11 for Sir Arthur and £100 for Dr. Sheridan). The net gain of Whig appointments is £27,516 (£10,005 in bishoprics; £9,030 in civil employments; and £8,436 in military commands). The difference between the Whig account and the Tory account is £27,405. The author quite accurately acknowledges that Lord Carteret does not have it within his power to bestow bishoprics, army commands, commissioners of revenue, and judgeships. However, he asserts that, except in cases in which persons are sent directly from England, the Lord Lieutenant's recommendations are regularly honored by the English Ministry. The "*only* considerable Station conferred on a reputed *Tory* since his present Excellency's Government, was" by appointment directly from England, and the author further acknowledges that in his calculations he has "allowed large Defalcations" for such appointments. In a masterful stroke of understatement, the author concludes, ". . . by a fair State of the Account; the Ballance, I conceive, *seems to lie* on the other Side."

Thus through extreme use of concession, through frequent statements which reflect a "proper" scorn and distrust of scholarship, and through incontestable mathematical calculations, Swift firmly establishes his ethical proof.

### DIMINUTION

The diminution in the essay is directed against two groups: the author's opposition, the Patriots; and scholarship and the scholarly man. This second diminution is closely related to the ethical proof, for it further demonstrates the author's good Whiggism; however, since it is more properly the device of diminution, it will be considered here. In this instance it is a device used in support of a larger device.

Lord Carteret was educated at Oxford, "whence, with a Singularity, scarce to be justified, he carried away more *Greek*, *Latin*, and *Philosophy*, than properly became a Person of his Rank. . . ." This education was the "Rock he split on"

when he came up to London. He continues to suffer under
these "Prejudices of a wrong Education," under "his old
*unfashionable* Academick Education," "this mistaken Method
of educating Youth in the Knowledge of antient Learning
and Language." It is therefore a great "Felicity" to this
kingdom that the sons of the gentry are of too tender a
constitution to suffer much reading and study. It is this
classical education which causes the Lord-Lieutenant to read
books in those "unknown" languages in his chambers and
in the House of Lords itself and to discuss such books at
table with "some *Book-learned* Companion" while "Persons
of *great Stations* are by." It would not, however, be dangerous
for the patriots to condescend in allowing Lord Carteret the
freedom to peruse these "exploded Readings." His Excellency
was even pleased to see school boys perform a play in Greek,
this peculiarity of Carteret being "A Thing never to be sufficiently wondered at." Lord Carteret is "a great Admirer" of
the Greek tongue "although for what Reasons I could never
imagine." Carteret's desire to reward scholars with preferments
arises from an "*antiquated* Notion, that good School-masters
ought to be encouraged in every Nation, professing Civility
and Religion."

Lord Carteret and Doctor Delany both had a "fatal Turn
of Mind towards *Heathenish* and *outlandish* Books and Languages. . . ." Sir Arthur Acheson is "reported to be an acknowledged *Tory;* and, what is almost as bad, a *Scholar* into the
Bargain." Nevertheless, it is true that he was awarded a small
government contract, "notwithstanding his *unfortunate* Principles, and his Knowledge in *Greek* and *Latin.*"

The diminution of scholarship and scholars accomplishes
two results: it substantiates the firm Whig principles of the
author, indicating as it does that he justly holds suspect this
out-moded education; and it operates with the large movement of concession which informs the whole essay. But the
author, for all his modernity, will not allow himself to swing
to the extreme element of his party. He therefore employs this
same device of diminution against the "Patriots," the zealots
of his own party, for it is they against whom he is defending
Lord Carteret.

Swift mixes diminution and open name-calling. The author

pretends pity for that "poor, angry, bustling, well-meaning Mortal *Pistorides*" for his excessive zeal in attacking opponents to the Whig party. That "miserable Creature *Traulus*" was also a man of too great party zeal. Swift insinuates sarcasm into his use of the word *patriots*, so that it too tends to be part of the name-calling. He moves into more exact diminution as he distinguishes between old Whigs like the author and the new Whig like Pistorides. The patriots should control such of their own members as Pistorides and Traulus and tolerate Whigs of "the *old fashioned Stamp*" who have both the country and the party more at heart. Men like Carteret should not "be stigmatized as *quondam* Tories by *Pistorides* and his Gang" simply because the Lord-Lieutenant enjoys conversing with men whose party affiliations are not clearly known. He should not be under ". . . Pain and Peril of displeasing the Zealots of his own Party; and thereby be put into a worse Condition than every common good Fellow; who may be a sincere *Protestant*, and a loyal Subject; and yet rather chuse to drink Ale at the *Pope's Head*, than muddy at the *King's*."

The author makes even clearer his diminution of *zeal* and *zealot* in the following paragraph:

It is certain, the high-flown Loyalists in the *present* Sense of the Word, have their thoughts, and Studies, and Tongues, so entirely diverted by political Schemes, that the Zeal of their *Principles* hath *eaten up* their *Understandings*; neither have they Time from their Employments, their Hopes, and their hourly Labours for acquiring new Additions of Merit, to amuse themselves with Philological Converse or Speculations which are utterly ruinous to all Schemes of rising in the World. (Paragraph 28).

One should pause a moment on Swift's use of the word *high-flown*. Swift uses the term "high-flyer" in the usual sense of naming the High Church segment of the Tory party (as in paragraphs 35 and 53). He has already (paragraph 12) called the famous Italian rope-dancer, Madam Violante, a "HIGH-FLYER," that "illustrious and dangerous Female" who is probably a "*Papist*" in her Heart." And here in the passage quoted above, Swift deftly takes the opposition's name for his own party and applies it to the opposition "in the *present* Sense of the Word," that sense being pejorative and connoting a person whose abstract speculations render him unfit for conduct in reality but who attempts concrete action with a grand airiness. The zealots have become so abstracted in speculations for ways and means of personal advancement that they have rendered themselves useless for any real service to the kingdom. When this "true Genius of Party once enters, it *sweeps the House clean,* and leaves room for many *other Spirits* to take joint Possession . . . ."

Possibly the most important single word in this line of diminution and name-calling occurs in paragraph thirty-nine, where the author calls the zealot Whigs *"Inquisitors."* Doctor Delany had received so many civilities from Queen Ann's appointee, Lord Chancellor Sir Constantine Phipps, that the author says, ". . . I doubt the Doctor never drank his Confusion since; and what makes the Matter desperate, it is now too late; unless our *Inquisitors* will be content with drinking *Confusion* to his *Memory.* . . ." Calling the Whig zealots *"Inquisitors"* fully establishes the character of the zealots and further implies the whole fearful and unreasonable situation of public affairs which both the moderate author and the Whig Lord-Lieutenant have been caught up in. Also it is quite important to notice that the word *inquisitors* interlocks this device of name-calling with the appeal to authority, for several of the author's authorities are spies and rumormongers such as inquisitors would employ and believe.

The diminution, coupled with name-calling, is very carefully manipulated. By diminishing scholarship, the author has at once demonstrated his own "untainted" education and somewhat mitigated Lord Carteret's education; and by diminishing the extreme segment of his own party, the author has the more firmly established the moderate position of Lord Carteret and of himself. In addition to these results, the author has been able to persuade pervasively through his vocabulary. Swift through this diminution and name-calling has erected a major member of the ironic structure, for the two devices indicate a value-system and this value-system partially determines and makes clear to the reader the ironic inversion. Further, Swift has managed to knit the fabric of his essay more tightly by interweaving diminution and name-calling with the ethical proof and with the appeal to authority.

### APPEAL TO AUTHORITY

As I have indicated earlier, Swift makes no pretense of preserving intact any "dramatic" *persona* which he creates. Since these essays have no dramatic quality in the sense that the "author" moves in a dramatic context, it is sometimes difficult to determine just when Swift stands at a great distance behind his author and when he slips forward and takes the pen from his author's hand. Swift's continually darting about behind and sometimes in front of his author makes the reader always aware of Swift's presence; it is characteristic of these ironical essays. Perhaps the appeal to authority in this essay is one of the best examples of this situation and of Swift's method. Swift has his author call forth appeals to authority on sixteen different occasions. The authorities are spies, general rumor, Hobbes, the curators of Bedlam, a story-book, and the majority opinion—all disreputable from Swift's point of view and possibly from the author's also. The author has made his distaste for spies and rumor-mongers clear enough in the essay; but, being a "modern," he might count Hobbes and the curators of Bedlam as real authorities. The main point is, however, that Swift achieves one of his strongest ironic strokes by undercutting the whole position he purports to defend by citing authorities which are ridiculous and which are the very authorities that the author's opponents would use and evidently have used. This accounts for the author's first using name-calling and diminution to brand the zealous Whigs as *"Inquisitors"* and establishing a milieu of distrust and spying and then his turning and citing such sources as his own authority. In confessing that Lord Carteret reads Latin and Greek books, he states, "For it is known, and can be proved upon him, that *Greek* and *Latin* Books might be found every Day in his Dressing-Room, if it were carefully searched; and there is Reason to suspect, that some of the said Books have been privately conveyed to him by *Tory* hands. I am likewise assured, that he hath been taken in the very Fact of reading the said Books. . . ." Sir Arthur Acheson is "reported to be an acknowledged *Tory*" and a scholar. And it "is whispered about, as a certain Truth, that this Gentleman is to have a Grant. . . ." ". . . I have it from good Hands. . . ." "NEITHER do I find any murmuring. . . ."

General knowledge informs the author concerning a particular principle in psychology. Arguing that it is impossible to excuse Traulus on the grounds of madness, the author answers, ". . . it is well known, that Madness only operates by inflaming and enlarging the good or evil Dispositions of the Mind. . . ." The general knowledge is quickly buttressed by specific medical authority: ". . . For the *Curators* of *Bedlam* assure us, that some Lunaticks are Persons" of honour and some of dishonour, each of which qualities simply becomes more pronounced in madness.

The author twice relies upon Hobbes as a specific authority: "as Hobbes wisely observes" and "Hobbes most judiciously observes."

In acknowledging that Lord Carteret is whimsical in his tastes for classical reading and the company of scholars, the author extenuates him by pointing out that other great men have also had their unaccountable little entertainments. These historical parallels the author draws from "old *English* Story-books," and he generously grants that the authority might not be reliable: "if it be true, what I have read in old *English* Story-books. . . ." Later in the paragraph he assures the reader of the present availability of the book: "Now I say, if these Facts be true, (and the Book where I found them is in Print) . . . ." Turning his appeal from the authority of this book to the general authority of the public, the author is confident that general opinion will support his contention that a few peculiar scholars of unknown party affiliation will not actually hurt the Lord-Lieutenant or his administration of Ireland:

. . . Still submitting my Opinion to that *happy Majority*, which I am confident is *always in the Right*; by whom the *Liberty* of the Subject hath been so frequently, so strenuously, and so successfully asserted; who, by their wise Councils, have made *Commerce* to flourish, *Money* to abound, Inhabitants to encrease, the Value of Land and Rents to rise; and the whole Island put on a new Face of *Plenty* and *Prosperity*.

With this magnificent *coup d'ironie* Swift has left his "authorities" in shreds, and it would seem that Swift and his author are one here, since this is the very kind of authority of rumor and the mob which has so unreasoningly attacked Lord Carteret. Just as in the Turning of the Charge, Swift has convicted his opponents out of their own mouths, so in his appeal to authority he has applied their own method and rendered it ridiculous. Rhetorically and ironically Swift's use of this device is one of the most effective in the essay and the most elaborate application of appeal to authority in all of these essays. Rhetorically it persuades by showing up the falseness of the source of the charge against Lord Carteret, and ironically his undercutting the device powerfully states to his opponents, "If these are your only sources of proof, you have no case." Further, in those instances in which the modern author seems sincerely to put forward one of these authorities, Swift can level the attack upon the moderate Whig author himself, convicting through guilt by association.

### PARENTHESIS

Swift's use of parenthesis in this essay, although somewhat extensive in contrast to its incidence in other of his ironical essays, is ostensibly orthodox: what pretends to be a casual aside contains, however, a strong ironic sting, so that the unobtrusive "tucking-in" quality of a parenthesis is heavily counterbalanced by the irony of the inserted comment. Swift uses these parentheses to reflect the modernity of the author, to convict him of sheer ignorance, to reinforce the arguments into which they are inserted, and to insert snide remarks to his auditors.

When the author states that Lord Carteret should be allowed his own private entertainments ". . . provided he gives no public Scandal (which is by all Means to be avoided) I say, why he may not be indulged twice a Week, to converse with one or two particular Persons . . . ," Swift tucks in the mocking parenthesis, in which he seems to echo his opponents' trite and petty attitude, as if they piously mouth this phrase over and over.

THUS I have, with the utmost Impartiality, collected every single Favour, (further than personal Civilities) conferred by his Excellency on *Tories*, and reputed *Tories* . . . .

What at first seems to be simply an aside inserted for clarity implies the author's opinion that some Whigs would confer upon a Tory the coldness of a civility only.

I AM well aware, how much my Sentiments differ from the *orthodox* Opinion of one or two principal Patriots, (at the Head of whom I name with Honour *Pistorides*.)

The effect of this parenthesis is to allow Swift an opening oblique attack instead of a frontal one, for libellers like Pistorides are severely attacked here in paragraphs ten and twelve, and quite heavily in paragraph thirteen. All of this attack the reader takes to be against Pistorides. However, it is not until paragraph fourteen that Swift flatly puts forth the case of Pistorides directly, where Pistorides is given four paragraphs of abuse. Thus, although there are actually only four paragraphs explicitly against him, Swift gains the effect of some seven paragraphs of abuse of this particular foe.

One parenthesis is used to insert a topical allusion which is not otherwise made use of and which is intended to cast aspersion upon the academic enemies of Dr. Delany:

THREE or four Years ago, the Doctor grown weary of an Academick Life, for some Reasons best known to the Managers of the Discipline in that learned Society (which it may not be to their Honour to mention), resolved to leave it . . . .

Scott's note to this passage states that when two undergraduates were expelled from Trinity College for alleged insolence to the Provost, Dr. Delany espoused their cause with such warmth that he too was compelled to acknowledge his "error" and to give full satisfaction to the College.

The author uses parenthesis to imply ignorance of his Whig auditors: "Now I say, if these Facts be true, (and the Book where I found them is in Print). . . ." In addition to his reinforcing the authority which he has already given, the author seems to say to his Whig auditors, "Astoundingly enough, this book really exists!"

Further indicating his generally concessive tone, the author at one point uses parenthesis to indicate that in small matters he freely admits to the possibility of error: "The second Gentleman (if I am right in my Chronology) . . . is Mr. *James Stopford* . . . ." With this possible sarcasm, the author also shows his contempt for the "facts" of such "inquisitorial" procedures as he is here forced to go into.

In paragraph thirty-two Swift uses parenthesis to tuck in further anticlassical bias of his modern Whig author. Having agreed with Hobbes that a classical education is politically dangerous, the author finds it to be a "great Felicity" that heirs to Irish estates and titles are of too weak a constitution to pursue these prolonged studies. As their mothers have said, they have not taken to their books but they are still sufficiently "Qualified to sign a Receipt for a Half a Year's Rent, to put their Name (*rightly spelt*) to a Warrant, to read Pamphlets against Religion and High-flying . . . ." In the next paragraph Swift increases this use of parenthesis in a running series of asides which help to establish the author as a real Modern with a "healthy" contempt for accuracy in antique matters—that is to say, with an utter ignorance of antique matters. Extended quotation will be necessary to show how these parentheses humorously break into the flow of the argument. The author is arguing that several great men of the past have had their peculiar pursuits; so why not indulge the Lord-Lieutenant in his pleasure in chatting with a few scholars:

Yet if it be true, what I have read in old *English* Story-books, that one Agesilaus (no Matter to the bulk of my Readers, whether I spell the names right or wrong) was caught by the *Parson of the Parish*, riding a Hobby-Horse with his ·Children; that *Socrates*, a Heathen Philosopher, was found dancing by himself at Fourscore; that a King called *Caesar Augustus* (or some such name) used to play with Boys; whereof· some might possibly be Sons of *Tories;* and that two great Men called *Scipio* and *Lelius*, (I forget their *Christian* Names, and whether they were Poets or Generals,) often played at *Duck and Drake*, with smooth Stones on a River.

The first parenthesis might initially be construed as a learned man's contempt for his readers; however, the subsequent parentheses, the rampant anachronisms, and the so completely nonessential appositives fully attest to the author's genuine Modernity.

The last use of parenthesis in the essay (paragraph 52) is perhaps the most important single one because it is brought into play at a point crucial to the essay as a whole. Through sustained diminution of the zealous Whigs the author has worked the argument around to the position that after all the only cases brought forth against Carteret are merely those of supposed Tories and that *real* Tories can with much greater ease be given appointments in England.

AND indeed it is but too remarkable, that, in a neighbouring Nation (where this dangerous Denomination of Men is incomparably more Numerous, more Powerful, and of consequence more Formidable) *real Tories* can often with much less Difficulty, obtain very high Favours from the Government, than their *reputed* Brethren can arrive to the lowest in ours.

Thus in this parenthesis a parallel argument is inserted which substantiates the reasons for the argument in the rest of the sentence: *because of* the number of English Tories, their power demands legitimate recognition as the Party of Loyal Opposition, a situation impossible in the more zealous Ireland.

### THE RHETORICAL QUESTION

Swift employs rhetorical question only twice, and in each instance he uses it in its classical function as simply a means of posing an argument (as opposed, e.g., to his use of it as a means of avoiding giving his argument where no good argument exists, as in his defence of Christianity).

The two questions are as follows:

. . . if Persons in high Stations have been allowed to chuse *Wenches*, without Regard even to Difference in Religion, yet never incurred the least Reflection on their Loyalty, or their Protestantism; shall the Chief Governor of a great Kingdom be censured for chusing a *Companion*, who may formerly have been suspected for differing from the *Orthodox* in some speculative Opinions of Persons and Things, which cannot affect the fundamental Principles of a sound *Whig*?

On the same subject the author asks what the Lord-Lieutenant is to do when all prospective conversationalists of his own party have through party zeal unfitted themselves as reasonable companions for Carteret: "What then must a great Man do, whose ill Stars have fatally perverted him to a Love, and Taste, and Possession of Literature, Politeness, and good sense?"

In both of these quotations Swift has managed not just to force from his reader an inevitable answer but to impress on his reader that the logic behind the questions renders any but the right answer to be inevitably foolish in the extreme.

## THE IRONIC STATEMENT AND ACCUMULATION

In this essay of complete ironic inversion almost every sentence is, of course, ironical—as in the quotation immediately above, and to comment upon each would prove tedious and insulting to the reader. However, given the ironic inversion, there are four ironic statements which the author uses within the broader inversion. Two are overstatements and two are understatements. The first understatement is a simple verbal irony already discussed as a parenthesis: ". . . (which it may not be to their Honour to mention) . . . ." The other ironical statements are of much greater significance.

Through his mathematical calculations the author has proved that if Sir Arthur Acheson is quite careful, he will be able to gain £11 from his contract to supply a barrack for the King or that, at the most, he can avoid going into debt:

However, I am confident he may with good Management be a *Saver* at least; which is a *prodigious Instance of Moderation* in our Friends towards a professed *Tory*, whatever Merit he may pretend by the Unwillingness he hath shewn to make his Excellency uneasy in his Administration.

Because the author depends so heavily upon moderation and concession, he has suppressed his irateness. Only in this and one other ironic overstatement does he allow his extreme exasperation to flash forth for a moment. His revealing his otherwise controlled anger strengthens the moderation and concession of the ethical proof through contrast and, more importantly, through thus indicating that the author has written his apology for Lord Carteret with tact and courtesy to zealous Whigs who might more deserve to be "anatomized" by that "political Surgeon," one of "that implacable Race of Wits."

The careful reader of Swift has come to realize that one of the hallmarks of Swift's ironic technique is the terrible and powerful undercutting of the final sections of sentences, paragraphs, and even whole essays (for example, the final paragraph of "A Modest Proposal") by a broad movement of anticlimax. He employs that technique to end this essay, saving a powerful understatement for the final sentence of the essay. The author calculates that Tory employments total £111 and that Whig employments total £27,516. He ends his essay with this sentence:

I SHALL conclude with this Observation, That, as I think, the *Tories* have sufficient Reason to be *fully satisfied* with the Share of *Trust*, and *Power*, and *Employments*, which they possess under the *Lenity* of the present Government: So, I do not find how his Excellency can be justly censured for favouring none but *High-Church, High-flyers, Termagants, Laudists, Sacheverelians, Tip-top-gallonmen, Jacobites, Tantivyes, Anti-Hanoverians, Friends to Popery and the Pretender, and to Arbitrary Power, Disobligers of England, Breakers of* DEPENDEN-CY, *Inflamers of Quarrels between the Two Kingdoms, Publick Incendiaries, Enemies of the King and Kingdoms, Haters of* TRUE *Protestants, Laurel-men, Annists, Complainers of the Nation's Poverty, Ormondians, Iconoclasts, Anti-Glorious-memorists, Anti-Revolutioners, White-rosalists, Tenth-a-Junians* and the like: When by a fair State of the Account; the Ballance, I conceive, *seems to lie* on the other Side.

In this sentence Swift combines several devices which operate mutually. Had he not carefully built his mathematical calculations up to the conclusion that there is a difference of £27,405 between the two totals, his understatement could not be made with such confidence: this huge disparity in money is translated directly into that disparity between real and apparent truth, which *is* irony. With this disparity so firmly fixed, he can afford to make his actual statement as slight as he cares to. On the one side he uses the device of accumulation to cluster twenty-five names or epithets for Tories. Against this he balances the overstatement that the Tories "have sufficient reason to be *fully satisfied*" and the understatement of characterizing his conclusion as simply his own "Observation" that the balance "*seems to lie* on the other Side." Added to these devices, the whole ethical proof is brought powerfully into play as the author somewhat tentatively and modestly offers what he conceives to be the proper conclusion to the question. Thus, the defence of Lord Carteret, which began in a tone of moderation and search for the truth, seems to come to rest in that same quiet tone of sweet moderation, but it actually is a conclusion charged with the electricity of ironic exposé.

## TURNING THE QUESTION

Most classical rhetoricians recommend that, where possible, one should turn his opponent's arguments and fling them back in his face. Swift has in this essay refined this rhetorical principle with astounding subtlety. Nowhere in the essay does he openly employ this device; rather, he "goes underground" to use it, at a level several degrees removed from the surface of his essay. The operation of the device is most easily seen through seeing the results of it. Swift, realizing that the Tory position is most frequently described as high-flying and offensively and overly conservatively orthodox, has thrown such epithets at his opponents and made them stick. He succeeds in making it appear that the author and Lord Carteret are the nonconformist exceptions. The effect is to rob the Whigs of their own position and to give them the unwanted position of reactionary and tyrannical orthodoxy. (These evaluations are based upon Whig values and the Whig political nomenclature.)

First we should examine the extensive occasions in which Swift has emphasized his definition of orthodox Whig and his insistent association of the zealous extremists with this definition. "I AM well aware, how much my Sentiments differ from the *orthodox* Opinion of one or two principal Patriots, (at the Head of whom I name with Honour *Pistorides*.)" He then states that the orthodoxy of such men has forced them to the staid rule that no man except a known Whig can come within the shadow of the castle. Later he argues that no harm will come to the kingdom if Carteret is allowed to entertain a few scholarly friends "who may formerly have been suspected for differing from the *Orthodox* in some speculative Opinions of Persons and Things, which cannot affect the fundamental Principles of a sound *Whig*." Pistorides, already established as a leader of this "Gang" of orthodox Whigs, is shown to be sick and mad, and Traulus (another of this "gang" of the orthodox) has his madness and foulness discussed at length (paragraphs 16-22). Traulus is substantially flayed and dissected alive, and has laid open to the view of mankind "the disordered Cells of his Brain, the Venom of his Tongue, the Corruption of his Heart, and Spots and Flatuses of his Spleen. . . ." The author has particularized for the world

. . . that unnatural Conjunction of Vices and Follies, so inconsistent with each other in the same Breast: Furious and fawning, scurrilous and flattering, cowardly and provoking, insolent and abject; most profligately false, with the strongest Professions of Sincerity; positive and variable, tyrannical and slavish.

Traulus is, quite simply, sick and mad. By stating that Pistorides and Traulus lead this Whig party, he implies that his descriptions of the leaders fit the whole party also. In paragraph twenty-eight he states as much when he describes the zeal-eaten minds of the Whigs: "It is certain, the high-flown Loyalists in the *present* Sense of the Word, have their thoughts, and Studies, and Tongues, so entirely diverted by political Schemes, that the *Zeal* of their *Principles* hath *eaten up* their *Understandings*. . . ." When "Genius of Party once enters, it *sweeps the House clean*. . . ." Thus, in such terms does Swift succeed in characterizing the brains of the orthodox Whig, the high-flying Whig. (Here one sees Swift again writing at fever pitch against his ancient enemies, zeal and madness, which he had long ago thoroughly flayed in *A Tale of a Tub*.)

It is against this orthodox Whig that the author must defend the nonorthodox Lord Carteret and himself, both moderate Whigs. The author manages to associate himself with the "*Whigs* in this Kingdom of the *old fashioned Stamp*" whose brains have not been so party-ridden that they cannot still take a detached view of the whole situation. As to Lord Carteret, the author freely admits that his education has been unorthodox, that Carteret's early adult life was not passed "according to Custom . . . losing his money in a Chocolate-House," and that his role as loving father and dutiful husband has not been according to the custom of lords and gentry. By insisting that such concessions of lack of orthodoxy do not lessen Carteret's principles as a "sound *Whig*," the author is able to label Carteret and himself as really liberal in the classical sense of that word and the more free-thinking, modern Whigs as the reactionary Orthodox. At one point he even attributes his description of the "orthodox" Whigs to the whole nation: "I COULD heartily wish his Excellency would be more condescending to the *Genius* of the Kingdom he governs. . ."—that is, Carteret is unorthodox in his whole situation in Ireland, not just in relation to the rest of his party members.

Thus in a few scattered, but well placed and carefully composed, paragraphs Swift has succeeded in completely switching the standard names, epithets, and descriptions of the parties. And he has done so without once admitting it overtly and without once employing this position as an argument at the argumentative level, although he becomes almost explicit in the final clause of the essay. This whole device gives added meaning and emphasis to the accumulation in the final paragraph of the essay. Reasonably pursued to its logical conclusion, the device clearly yields this further deduction: Swift's author is able to imply the grand foolishness of the whole complaint against Lord Carteret through his showing that the complainers are the high-flying orthodox who are violently upset when the Lord-Lieutenant awards a few employments to the high-flying orthodox.

### Conclusions

Through a carefully sustained ethical proof Swift has established an author of such seeming mildness and fairness that his reader is disposed to accept his arguments as reasonable and just. The seemingly endless concessions which the author makes testify to his fairness; his unselfconsciously reflecting his "sound *Whig*" principles makes his essay comfortable to his Whig audience; his frankness in discussing those very cases deemed to be the most damaging to Lord Carteret bespeaks his fearlessness in his position of right; his long classical digression isolates, attacks, and reveals the segment of the party opposed to Lord Carteret (and to the author himself), and that attack is telling since most of the essay is ostensibly defensive. Coupled with these several aspects of the ethical proof is the diminution of scholarship and the scholar, which reinforces the ethical proof by further indicating the author's "good" Whig and "modern" qualities.

Having clearly characterized the opposition in the digression, the author employs diminution of these extreme Whig Patroits until they are little more than "Pistorides' Gang," who are the narrowest and most myopic of all the orthodox: they are the "Inquisitors" whose nationalistic zeal has no place in a free society of scholars such as Lord Carteret.

Although Swift joins with his author in an ostensible appeal to authority, Swift always and his author evidently most of the time undercut the whole appeal to the authority of the curators of Bedlam, Hobbes, spies, rumor, old English story-books, and the majority opinion—that great reservoir of right thinking. This severe ironic undercutting, as we have seen, renders ridiculous the sources of the charges against Lord Carteret. Swift's constant lurking behind and his sometimes standing right beside or in front of his author is a major means by which these ironical essays gain in ironic intensity and variety. This is the salient fact; and, when in this exploration of the irony attempts are made to ascertain which statements are the author's and which are Swift's, I do so only to examine the complexity of the irony and to establish the degree and direction of the irony through suggesting the point of view from which it springs. Therefore, in reference to his author, the effect of Swift's manipulation of the appeal to authority in this essay is to render the author a somewhat muddle-headed modern who uses the appeal falsely in order to show up his opponents' illegitimate use of the device (here, he and Swift coincide) but who also, as a modern and as a Whig, might be inclined to treat Hobbes and the specialists at Bedlam as real authorities. Thus the author convicts himself by using his own false rhetoric.

Swift uses parenthesis to insert sarcasm against his Whig auditors, to indicate the ignorance of his modern author, and to reinforce by implied parallel arguments the arguments into which parenthetic comments are inserted. In one important passage near the end of the essay he succeeds through parenthesis (in his reference to the *real* Tories in England) to render all arguments against Lord Carteret phantom-like in contrast to the real appointments of many real and powerful Tories in England. This reducing in one stroke of vocabulary a whole argument to a mere question of nominalism is reminiscent of the powerful conclusion to his essay against abolishing Christianity, in which he accomplishes the same end by the same means.

The author's otherwise finely controlled anger is allowed to burst forth only twice, in two ironic overstatements, reflecting once more the reasoned calmness and mildness of the author against opponents whom he has proved to be unworthy of such a noble opponent.

By an extremely careful control of vocabulary and the current connotations of names and epithets, Swift, following an ancient trick of rhetoric, succeeds in convicting the Whig zealots out of their own mouths: they become the offensive high-flying orthodox.

And in the final paragraph Swift amasses his rhetorical devices with a care and concentration amazing even in Swift. The mathematical proof of his contention, the angry overstatement, accumulation, the reversing of the epithets, the modesty and reasonableness of the author—all of these are balanced against—only to be overbalanced by—the slender reed of a quiet understatement, "the Ballance, I conceive, *seems to lie* on the other Side."

## CHAPTER V

# "The Answer to the *Craftsman*"

SWIFT wrote "A Modest Proposal" late in 1729, and during the following winter, he had occasion to write "The Answer to the *Craftsman*," an ironical essay admittedly written by the "author" of the proposal. Again the author "humbly" puts forward a proposal for the betterment of Ireland at no expense to England: part of the annual crop of young Irishmen should be exported by whatever prince will "bear the Carriage."

In the winter of 1730 several French officers, under permission granted by the English Crown, established themselves in Dublin to recruit Irishmen for the armies of the French king, who so late had been England's enemy and who was to be so again in the not very distant future. Quite naturally, Swift greatly disapproved of the granting of such permission, as did even some of the Irish Whig apologists for the English policy. The Tory *Craftsman* printed an ably written and well argued essay disapproving of the use of Irish troops in the French army and especially of the English Government's making such recruiting so simple for the French and for the Irish.[1] This author points out that, alarming as the number of such Irish troops is, the French system of maintaining them in separate Irish regiments is an even graver threat to the Protestant Succession because these Roman Catholic English subjects in the pay of the French king and the Pretender could serve to encourage rebellion in England and Ireland in a way that foreigners could not. He also points out that, in addition to the Irish officers of these regiments, the noncommissioned officers form a well-trained cadre which could quickly be expanded into a staff of field grade officers for rapid enlargement of these Irish regiments into well-staffed armies. He states that the procedure is patently illegal, for the Irish Code makes it a felony for any subject to enlist or to cause others to enlist in the service of any foreign prince. Furthermore, if the English king this one time allow the raising of French troops in Ireland, how will the poor Irish illiterates know in the future whether they sign up with frauds who merely pretend to have the English king's permission? If the English king grant this permission to the French king, it is likely that his *"Catholick Majesty"* of Spain might demand equal rights and thus make refusal a pretense for war to capture Gibraltar. The sad state of the Irish economy has already forced many of her people to emigrate, and she can hardly afford this further drain upon her population. This license would encourage the Irish to continue to be Roman Catholics, for they could always count upon service in the French army and possibly in the Spanish. The English should consider that these Irish troops of the French king have often been used to argue for the presence of a standing army in England, a Whig innovation which few Englishmen cared for. The author then addresses himself to minor practical considerations, such as the question whether French martial law will supersede Irish law within these newly formed groups of the French army while they remain resident in Ireland.

At only one point in this essay does the author allow himself to wax ironical. Referring to this English permission given the French, he writes:

Such a Method of providing for Persons, whose Principles render them unserviceable in *our Army*, is indeed a little more charitable than a *late Project* for preventing *Irish Children* from being starv'd, by fattening them up and selling them to the *Butcher*.

This obviously is an invitation to Swift to resume his pose as the modest proposer; he accepts the "challenge" and opens his "Answer" by taking literally the ironical sentence from the *Craftsman's* essay:

You are pleased to reflect on a Project I proposed of making the Children of *Irish* Parents to be useful to the Publick instead of being burthensome; and you venture to assert, that your own Scheme is more charitable, of not permitting our Popish Natives to be listed in the Serivce of any foreign Prince.

## THE ETHICAL PROOF

Swift's manipulation of the ethical proof in this essay is radically different from his use of this kind of proof in the other ironical essays. Except for a few passages in which his author condescends to appear humble, Swift virtually abandons all humility. However, he does not abandon reasonableness: the new scheme which he is recommending is as "reasonable" as the earlier proposal, for each point easily passes the acid test that it is at once beneficial to British interests and to Irish interests. Swift relies heavily in this essay upon establishing the ethical proof through evidence of careful consideration and through mathematical proof, and, although this essay must of course stand on its own merits, Swift, having so deliberately identified it as coming from the same hand as that of "A Modest Proposal," can reasonably assume that the ethical proof of that essay might be carried over into this essay. The author, having appeared to be so gracious and humble in "A Modest Proposal," has subsequently been attacked and challenged with impertinent objections. In his "Answer," then, he appears as the angered polemicist:

Sir, I detest reading your Papers, because I am not of your Principles, and because I cannot endure to be convinced. Yet, I was prevailed upon to peruse your CRAFTSMAN of *December* the 12th, wherein I discover you to be as great an Enemy of this Country, as you are of your own.

The vocabulary of succeeding paragraphs continues this saucy and somewhat belligerent tone: "You are pleased to reflect on"; "you venture to assert"; "Perhaps, Sir, you may not have heard"; "you are pleased, without a Call, officiously and maliciously to interpose with very frivolous Arguments"; "Yet this very Grace and Favour [permission to draft Irishmen into the French armies] you, *Mr. D'Anvers*, whom we never disobliged, are endeavoring to prevent." Such language, with its *argumentum ad hominem*, is dropped after paragraph three, for the author indicates by his silence from this point forward on the subject that he has no noble enemy and disdains traffic with any other kind. After he moves into the main body of his discourse, the author forgets all about that rather foolish "*Mr. D'Anvers*," who had provoked him into print.

Were this initial burst of anger the main or prevailing element of the ethical proof, that proof could hardly sustain its proper rhetorical function. But Swift very carefully shifts the real basis of the ethical proof to the accurateness and reliability of the author, whose historical research and mathematical proof attest to these qualities in him. Thus, the angry tones of the first few paragraphs, far from detracting from the ethical proof, reinforce it by indicating the immense justification for this great projector's having been vexed. And, of course, the element of condescension in the opening remarks implies the author's position of superiority.

The author's careful consideration of his scheme is indicated in two ways: by his researches into the history of the problem and by his mathematics. On the one topic which the author has not fully thought out, he readily admits he has little but first impressions to offer, and he limits these comments to one brief paragraph: "As to the Civil and Ecclesiastical Administration, which I have not yet fully considered, I can say little."

He establishes the historical background in paragraph three. About sixty years ago, he says, the English Parliament prohibited the Irish exportation of live cattle.[2] Having found that such an inflexible policy did not always work to the benefit of England, the English Parliament, when it considered a bill to prohibit the "exportation of live men" from Ireland, wisely inserted a clause granting permission to do so upon the signed order of the king. In paragraph four the author brings the situation up to the present state of affairs: the French king now (as the Spanish king might be subsequently) has been granted such permission by King George. In the whole recent history of Irish exportation of flesh, the one loop-hole left to the Irish has at last been opened by the king; so, why should the *Craftsman* assume so anti-Irish an attitude as to deny Ireland the one chance she has for exporting some of her native flesh?

Indeed, the whole basis of the main scheme being proposed is historical. The proposal, simply stated, is that England should assume her rightful duty (and "burden") of supplying Ireland with all manufactured articles, thus freeing the Irish to return to their "historical," purely Arcadian bliss, in which they could while away their days tending their sheep while the poor English did all the hard work: ". . . so that the industrious

Shepherd and Cow-herd may sit, every Man under his own
Blackberry Bush, and on his own Potatoe-Bed, whereby this
happy Island will become a new *Arcadia*."³

A collateral proposal is that Ireland should abandon the
"modern" English "Trade of Bankers" and return to the
simpler method of payment in kind. If a few coins of mean
worth be needed, let them be made of leather and stamped
in England. After all, bartering is the ancient method of commerce; money and banking are modern innovations which
have occupied their little space in history for an extremely
short period of time. History testifies to the superiority of
the ancient practice.

The history of the relationship between the two countries
further substantiates the inherent rights of England:

THIS Expedient will be of great Advantage to both Kingdoms,
upon several Accounts: For, as to *England*, they have a just
Claim to the Balance of Trade on their Side with the whole
World; and therefore our Ancestors and we, who conquered
this Kingdom for them, ought to let them have the whole
Benefit of their Conquest to themselves; especially, when the
Conquest was amicably made, without Bloodshed, by a Stipu-
lation between the *Irish* Princes and *Henry* II. by which they
paid him, indeed, not equal Homage with what the Electors of
Germany do to the Emperor, but very near the same that he did
to the King of *France* for his *French* Dominions.

Pretending that the English misconception of the Irish as
"the savage old Irish" (a misconception famous as early as
Spenser's time) is historically accurate, the author informs his
English readers that the Irish, having become more humane,
are suitable now to return to the beautiful simplicity of antiquity:

. . . to which Employments [shepherding and limited farming]
they are turned by Nature, as descended from the *Scythians*,
whose Diet they are still so fond of. So *Virgil* describeth it:
*Et lac concretum cum sanguine bibit equino.*
Which, in *English*, is Bonnyclabber [thick, sour milk],
mingled with the Blood of Horses, as they formerly did, until
about the Beginning of the last Century Luxury, under the Form
of Politeness, began to creep in, they changed the Blood of
Horses for that of their black Cattle; and by Consequence, be-

came less war-like than their Ancestors. [During the famine years the Irish did actually bleed their cattle and mix the blood with milk for nourishment.]

Thus the historical acumen of the author and his ready knowledge of the history of the two kingdoms and its application to the present question contribute to the ethical proof, which part of the proof is alone more than sufficient to counterbalance the testy manner of the opening paragraphs. But Swift does not let the ethical proof rest on this one basis. He substantiates it more elaborately in the mathematical proof for his scheme of the new Arcadia.

The projector first gives the background figures for the Irish inbalance of trade. Since the traffic in flesh is the basis of the new commerce which he is urging, he refers to the birth of an Irishman as an "import," and sending the Irish to the French army as an "export":

PERHAPS Sir, you may not have heard of any kingdom so unhappy as this, both in their Imports and Exports. We import a Sort of Goods, of no intrinsick Value, which costeth us above Forty Thousand Pounds a Year to dress, and scour, and polish them, which altogether do not yield one Penny Advantage; and we annually export above Seven Hundred Thousand Pounds a Year in another Kind of Goods, for which we receive not one single Farthing in Return: Even the Money paid for the Letters sent in transacting this Commerce being all returned to *England*. But now, when there is a most lucky Opportunity offered to begin a Trade, whereby this Nation will save many Thousand Pounds a Year, and *England* be a prodigious Gainer, you are pleased, without a Call, officiously and maliciously to interpose with very frivolous Arguments.

Assuming that the upkeep of a "tall, hungry, *Irish* Man" is five pounds per year, then if the kings of Spain and France carry off only 6,000 per year, £30,000 annually will be saved. And if perchance, these "Potentates" carry 30, 40, or 50 thousand, the savings will obviously spiral upwards.[4] At best, this part of the plan is only negative: no profit can be made (for England reaps the profit); great savings, however, can be realized.

The projector is now ready to lay the mathematical groundwork for his Arcadian scheme. The "profitable Land" of the kingdom is reckoned at 17 million acres, all of which the author proposes be turned into grazing. One grazier and his family can manage 2,000 acres. Thus, 16,800,000 acres can easily be managed by 8,400 families, and the fraction of acres difference will be more than sufficient for "Cabbins, Out-Houses, and Potatoe-Gardens. . . ."

These 8,400 families can be divided among the four provinces according to the number of houses already existing in the provinces. Making allowance for eight members to a family, there will be 67,200 "souls." Added to these will be the British standing army of 20,000 English, plus their "Trulls, their Bastards, and their Horse-Boys," the latter of which will raise the English non-graziers to a number equal to the graziers, thus resulting in two equal groups which can effectively defend and graze the country. In working out these figures, Swift makes an oblique attack upon the existence of a standing army in Ireland, and more especially upon its size. For if the English army in Ireland numbers only 20,000, then their "Trulls, their Bastards, and their Horse-Boys" number 47,200. Swift leaves us to assume that the non-military part of the whole English establishment is composed of trulls, bastards, and horse-boys. Further attacking the standing army, Swift has his projector observe that this army, lacking any real employment, may be busied with the job of tax collecting—no small job, indeed, for in this new Arcadia taxes will be rendered in kind.

The projector's motive for bestirring himself to answer the *Craftsman* and for putting forward his counter-proposal is the highest possible one for the public orator: love of country and concern for its welfare. Just as the mathematical and historical background material in the essay are at once part of the ethical proof and of the reasons urged for adopting the proposal, so the extensive evidence of the projector's patriotism serves simultaneously to create the ethical proof and to substantiate one of the main reasons for adopting the proposal: the projector has hit upon a scheme which peculiarly and at every point serves the interest of both England and Ireland, and he can therefore double the strength of the ethical proof by being both a loyal Englishman and a loyal Irishman:

UPON this Occasion, I desire humbly to offer a Scheme,

which, in my Opinion, would best answer the true Interests of both Kingdoms: For, although I bear a most tender, filial Affection to *England*, my dear, native Country; yet, I cannot deny but this noble Island hath a great Share in my Love and Esteem, nor can I express how much I desire to see it flourish in Trade and Opulence, even beyond its present happy Condition.

Swift begins this part of the ethical proof in the opening paragraph of the essay by immediately establishing the fact that the writer for the *Craftsman* is a traitor to both England and Ireland—to the former by attempting to cut off a source of her rightful trade and to the latter by attempting to cut off her only outlet of trade: "Yet, I was prevailed on to peruse your CRAFTSMAN of *December* the 12th, wherein I discover you to be as great an Enemy of this Country, as you are of your own." The accusation is continued in paragraph three: "Yet this very Grace and Favour you, Mr. *D'Anvers*, whom we never disobliged, are endeavouring to prevent; which, I will take upon me to say, is a manifest Mark of your Disaffection to his Majesty, a Want of Duty to the Ministry, and a wicked Design of oppressing this Kingdom, and a traiterous Attempt to lessen the Trade and Manufacture of *England*." Of course, by implication, the projector who opposes such a person is the opposite of this kind of man. Since Mr. D'Anvers is a traitor to both England and Ireland, one is left wondering to whom he is loyal, for we are told that he is not merely a misguided patriot: he has deliberately and maliciously set himself against the exportation of this new product.

Having set himself the rhetorical task of sustaining this double loyalty in his Anglo-Irish projector, Swift accomplishes his goal with grace and ease. His main method lies in the definition of the phrase quoted above: "the true Interests of both Kingdoms." It is the unparalleled good fortune of Ireland that her destiny is for her to revert to that purer society of ancient and poetic Arcadia, and that at this juncture in history her gracious neighbor England has as a part of her destiny the responsibility of supplying Ireland with food and manufactured items which are produced by hard work and the unpleasant features of modernism and industrialism. The Irish shepherd can sport with Amaryllis in the shade while his

English brothers toil. But only apparently so, for Swift has set up a perilous balance of double irony. At the same time that he pretends to sketch the "romantic" Hibernian Arcadia, he burlesques the traditional pastoral setting by substituting a blackberry bush for the classical hawthorn or laurel, and a potato-bed for the gently flowing stream. Swift gives a picture of a little Irishman huddled under an entangling bush the leaves of which have a prickly fuzz and the stems of which have briers. The ironic point here is apt, for the burlesquing indicates Swift's view that a completely agrarian insular country could not survive in a century of mercantilism and growing industry. At every point that he refers to this New Arcadia, he adjusts his tone and vocabulary to pretend to a somewhat bucolic tenderness: "Every Man under his own Blackberry Bush, and on his own Potatoe-Bed, whereby this happy Island will become a new *Arcadia*." As is his wont, Swift momentarily breaks through his *persona* to burlesque ironically the logical conclusion of the British policy—i.e., that Ireland is to be one great English plantation of limited agricultural products. This double-play of irony should be attributed to Swift and not to this author, who does not consciously employ irony. After this sentence Swift retires and has his author continue.

The projector, fearing possibly that some of the English might become jealous of this joyous state of Ireland, becomes slightly pro-Irish: "*England* should be forced, at their own Rates, to send us over Cloaths ready made, as well as Shirts and Smocks to the Soldiers and their Trulls; all Iron, Wooden, and Earthen Ware; and whatever Furniture may be necessary for the Cabbins of Graziers, with a sufficient Quantity of Gin, and other Spirits, for those who can afford to get drunk on Holydays." Because of the just agreement between the Irish princes and King Henry II, this proposed arrangement between England and Ireland fulfills the ends of justice, for England's claims over the Irish economy are right and just, and by implication Ireland's demand for manufactured supplies is also just and right: in consequence of this rightful precedence which England has in Ireland, England "may very reasonably demand the Benefit of all our Commodities in their natural Growth, to be manufactured by their People, and a sufficient Quantity of them for our Use to be returned hither fully manufactured."

This perfect dove-tailing of the economies of the two kingdoms will be further enhanced by the peace which will result between the two:

THAT which maketh me more zealously bent upon this Scheme, is my Desire of living in Amity with our neighboring Brethren; for we have already tried all other Means, without Effect, to that blessed End: And, by the Course of Measures taken for some years past, it should seem that we are all agreed in the Point.

Balanced against this Irish patriotism of the projector is his equally strong loyalty to his "dear native Country" England. This new Irish commerce will render England a "prodigious Gainer," for not only will she reap the payment for this exported commodity but also she will collect for the letters patent which will be issued for such transactions. England will profit in the inbalance of trade, for Ireland will be relieved of the onus of responsibility. The English will also have the responsibility of administering the agrarian society, only the Irish being so fortunate as to be carefree shepherds. England will further gain by the necessity of sending the managers back to England to spend their money: "I ADVISE, that all the Owners of these Lands should live constantly in England, in order to learn Politeness, and qualify themselves for Employments. . . ." From the Irish point of view these heavy responsibilities are a burden; however, from the English point of view they are not, because, for some reason, Englishmen enjoy this kind of thing: therefore both are to be satisfied.

Thus, by having evolved a scheme which at once satisfies both the English and the Irish, the projector can at once be both perfect Irish patriot and loyal Englishman. This situation gives redoubled force to this element of the ethical proof, a force which is not so arrived at in the ethical proofs which Swift employs in other ironical essays.

The projector, having shown himself in "A Modest Proposal" to be slow to anger, returns to the battle to answer the *Craftsman*, bursts out in righteous indignation at having to answer such foolish arguments, but after only a few outbursts of personal attack settles to his task of introducing yet another all-encompassing plan for the good of Ireland. His writing reflects the careful reading which prepared him in the background of the problem. His extensive mathematical calculations, in addition to functioning as a proof, reflect the intelligent and careful computations upon which the scheme is to rest. And his great love for both his adopted land and his motherland springs forth on every page of his essay and thus attests to his great motive for returning to print.

The only time that he admits being zealous occurs when he is emphasizing the wonderful friendship which will grow from the peace which will be established between the two kingdoms: "THAT which maketh me more zealously bent upon this Scheme, is my Desire of living in Amity with our neighbouring Brethren; for we have already tried all other Means, without Effect, to that blessed End."

## DIMINUTION

The diminution of the people of Ireland is essential for the author to support his scheme, for they must roughly be equated to cattle, the article of export in this scheme. The device, as applied here, functions simultaneously as diminution and as parody on the economic projectors whose wont was to treat people as ciphers, as cattle. Further, the device is a means of Swift's making the satiric point that the English Parliament also tends to treat the Irish as so many head of cattle.

The diminution begins in paragraph two, where the author explains that "We import a Sort of Goods, of no intrinsick Value, which costeth us above Forty Thousand Pounds a Year to dress, and scour, and polish them, which altogether do not yield one Penny Advantage. . . ." This import which has no intrinsic value is, of course, human beings; and, although one doesn't usually think of polishing them, the verbs *to dress* and *to scour* easily apply. But these last two words also apply with quite a different meaning to cattle; Swift takes full advantage of this word play. The diminution continues in the next paragraph. The author summarizes the recent history of Ireland's commerce in reference to the "Exportation of live Cattle," pointing out that when the English Parliament passed a bill to prohibit the "Exportation of live Men to any foreign Country," the Parliament wisely left the provision

that such could be done under letters patent signed by the
King. To oppose this provision is "a traiterous Attempt to
lessen the Trade and Manufacture of *England*." Swift accomplishes this easy shift in diminution by repetition of exact
phrases: "the Exportation of live cattle" becomes "the Exportation of live men." The force of the historical sketch of
the problem is to focus the reader's attention on the one
similarity which exists between the two products: both are
live flesh, each of which is being "exported" with as little
ceremony as the other.

Just as in "A Modest Proposal," Swift accomplishes the
diminution to the animal term not by recourse totally to the
animal term until one forgets that human beings are involved,
but by the constant varying of the term until the animal term
appears to be just as "normal" as the human term: from the
author's point of view, it little matters what we call these
people, just so we call them some word which clearly denotes
them. In paragraph four the neutral term is used in conjunction
with the human term: "OUR truest and best Ally the most
Christian King hath obtained his Majesty's Licence, pursuant
to Law, to export from hence some Thousand Bodies of
healthy, young, living Men, to supply his *Irish* Regiments."
The permission for this whole transaction is merely a "Civility," which the Spanish king might also expect from the
English king. In the following sentence the human term is used
("Man"), followed immediately by the mixed terminology:
". . . by computing the Maintenance of a tall, hungry, *Irish*
Man, in Food and Cloaths, to be only at Five Pounds a Head,
here will be Thirty Thousand Pounds *per Annum* saved clear
to the Nation, for they can find no other Employment at
Home beside begging, robbing, or stealing."

Sending these men out to fight and possibly to die for
the French king (who continues really to be England's
enemy) is merely an "Errand": "But, if Thirty, Forty, or
Fifty Thousand, (which we could gladly spare) were sent
on the same Errand, what an immense Benefit must it be to
us." These human beings who remain in Ireland become, in
the economic projector's term, "Hands": by such a practice,
"the Lands of *Ireland* that want Hands for Tillage" must
be employed in grazing.

In the paragraphs in which the mathematical basis of the scheme is laid, the Irish are referred to not by the inhuman term but merely by the nonhuman neutral term: "Grazier," "Family," "Inhabitants," "Souls." Within the context of the paragraph, a context which is heavily sociological in its statistical treatment of human beings, these words are neutral. However, as will be discussed below, these same words are subtly manipulated into one of the strands of amplification.

When the author suggests that the number of graziers can be kept at a statistical constant by exporting the excess, his terms are these: "But, for Fear of increasing the Natives in this Island, [I recommend] that an annual Draught, according to the Number born every Year, be exported to whatever Prince will bear the Carriage; or transplanted to the *English* Dominions on the *American* Continent, as a Screen between his Majesty's *English* Subjects and the savage *Indians*."

The author returns to the neutral terms in paragraph fifteen, referring to the Irish as "our Inhabitants the Graziers"; then, by recalling the practice of their ancestors, the Scythians, of drinking a mixture of blood and milk, he emphasizes their animality—mitigated only by the modern Irishmen's substituting the blood of their black cattle for that of horses, which was formerly used.

In the final paragraph of the essay occurs a wholly new diminution: the Irish are frankly called "Slaves." The Irish, he says, are already beginning to discard the modern "Trade of Bankers" and reverting to the ancient and more honorable practice of bartering: the result is that " 'Squires turn Tenants to themselves, divide so many Cattle to their Slaves, who are to provide such a Quantity of Butter, Hides, or Tallow, still keeping up their Number of Cattle; and carry the Goods to *Corke*, or other Port-Towns, and then sell them to the Merchants." In this final item of the diminution the word *slaves* is thrust upon the audience, thus explicitly undercutting the amplification, and even the diminution. If this is a single-word breakthrough on Swift's part, the result is that Swift indicates, through dropping his pose behind his projector and leaping beyond the now-hampering bounds of ironic artistry, that he has reached the climax of the diminution and that accurate statement of it lies only beyond the rhetorical rules. However, it is not at all clear that Swift interrupts his projector in this passage. If it is the projector who calls these Irishmen "Slaves," the result is even more devastating, for his using the word indicates that to him it is a perfectly "normal" term which in no way is a breach of his diminution.

Although the author employs amplification in his treatment of the English, he smuggles in diminution in his references to the English establishment in Ireland. The English exploitation of Ireland is *not* a part of the diminution, for the author freely grants that England has a "right" to all the produce of Ireland. The statement that half of the population of the kingdom is the English army and the English administrative establishment is a part of this diminution: ". . . to these we are to add a Standing Army of Twenty Thousand *English*, which, together with their Trulls, their Bastards, and their Horse-Boys, will, by a gross Computation, very near double the Count," i.e., the population of Ireland. One of these words is repeated in paragraph nine: the English must be forced to send over at their own rates "Cloaths ready made, as well as Shirts and Smocks to the Soldiers and their Trulls."

## AMPLIFICATION

The use of amplification in this essay is subtle and complex, although its operation is not therefore difficult to observe. The more customary use of diminution and amplification is for a writer to employ the one on one side of an argument and the other on the opposite side with the result that the two devices operate together by operating against each other and thus create the largest possible gap between the highly praised and the highly degraded. Because in this particular essay Swift has managed to identify completely the Irish and the English interests, he is able to set these two devices into an entirely new relationship: both the Irish and the English positions can be amplified without any contradictions. Characterizing the two sides in general terms, one can say that the Irish position is praised for the wonderfully Arcadian way of life which will result from the execution of this scheme and that the English position is praised for England's great, although burdensome, destiny of being the manufacturer for her colonies and allied kingdoms and for being the natural seat of a sophisticated culture.

The English position is amplified in the following terms. We "are infinitely obliged to the *British* Legislature." The author bears a "filial Affection to *England*, my dear, native Country." "I ADVISE, that all the Owners of these Lands [the Irish grazing lands] should live constantly in *England*, in order to learn Politeness, and qualify themselves for Employments." "I ADVISE likewise, that no Commodity whatsoever, of this Nation's Growth, should be sent to any other Country, except *England*, under the Penalty of high Treason; and that all the said Commodities shall be sent in their natural State. . . ." "I DO likewise propose, that no Money shall be used in *Ireland*, except what is made of Leather, which likewise shall be coined in *England*, and imported; and that the Taxes shall be levied out of the Commodities we export to *England*, and there turned into Money for his Majesty's Use; and the Rents to Landlords discharged in the same Manner." "Amity with our neighbouring Brethren," the English, is one of the main motives for the author's putting forth his scheme.

The use of money and the "Trade of Bankers" is disparagingly spoken of by the author; however, this tone does not detract from the English. The attitude of the author is that the innovation of money is a modern evil which Ireland, that happy land, luckily can avoid but which England, being a great manufacturing power, can easily benefit from. Payment in kind "will be no Manner of Grievance; for we already see it very practicable to live without Money, and shall be more convinced of it every Day. But whether Paper shall still continue to supply that Defect, or whether we shall hang up all those who profess the Trade of Bankers, (which latter I am rather inclined to) must be left to the Consideration of wiser Politicians." This topic is the subject of the concluding paragraph:

ALTHOUGH I proposed that the Army should be Collectors of the publick Revenues, yet I did not thereby intend that those Taxes should be paid in Gold or Silver, but in kind, as all other Rent: For the Custom of Tenants making their payments in Money, is a new Thing in the World little known in former Ages, nor generally practiced in any Nation at present, except this Island, and the Southern Parts of *Britain*.

The amplification of the Irish position, far from being at

odds with this amplification, runs quite compatibly along-side it. There is one exception. As the essay opens, it would appear that the English and Irish interests are in conflict, the impression being due in part to the natural pre-conception which the reader brings to his first reading of the essay. But as soon as the author makes the identification of the Irish and English interests, this apparent conflict is dissolved. Since it has already been demonstrated that diminution is em-ployed against the Irish, one might easily ask how it is that both amplification and diminution can be used against the same object simultaneously. The answer is that more than one group of Irish is involved, and from more than one point of view. The group to be exported is treated callously by the economic (English) projector as so many cattle; the group left to become happy shepherds has its position ironically amplified. Swift's adroitness in this particular amplification is the more to be marveled at when one recalls that the same device is also in operation on the other side of the argument. Swift has very carefully kept completely lucid the several points of view which inform the several patterns of the amplification.

There is one point in the essay where the diminution and the amplification of the Irish meet and, almost unaccountably, blend. It is paragraph seven, already referred to in this con-nection. The economic projector refers to the prospective graziers as "THESE Eight Thousand Four Hundred Families," "the Number of Inhabitants," "Sixty Seven Thousand Two Hundred Souls." The words *families, inhabitants*, and *souls* are, in context, the sociologist's jargon and as such should be taken as diminution to the neutral term. At the same time, however, these words are also beginning the amplification of the Irish shepherds, for the word *families* in addition to naming a statistical unit also connotes a valued human re-lationship, and *souls* has a pathetic force because the word both connotes a spiritual entity and is also a means of dis-tinguishing statistically between human and nonhuman ani-mals. From this paragraph forward the "new *Arcadia*" is subtly burlesqued in what looks at first like flattery: ". . . the industrious Shepherd and Cow-herd may sit, every Man under his own Blackberry Bush, and on his own Potatoe-Bed,

whereby this happy Island will become a new *Arcadia*."
There will be no industrialism, no corrupting commerce
(except the exportation of this new flesh, but that will be
carried on at only a few port towns). There will be no com-
plications of money. The benefit will be great because there
will be no time to engage in industry and commerce anyway,
". . . our Inhabitants the Graziers, when Time and Labour
will be too much taken up in manuring their Ground, feed-
ing their Cattle, sheering their Sheep, and sending over their
Oxen fit for Slaughter; to which employments they are turned
by Nature, as descended from the Scythians . . . ."

This "idyllic" picture of Ireland is sustained until the
last paragraph of the essay, where for a moment either Swift
(completely lifting the ironic veil) or the projector (using
a term perfectly "normal" to him) flatly calls these Irish
shepherds "Slaves." But, after dropping that one word *slaves*,
he returns with an even more powerful ironic thrust, more
powerful because it immediately follows its most real contrast: "By which Invention [bartering] there is no such Thing
as a ruined Farmer to be seen; but the People live with Comfort on Potatoes and Bonnyclabber, neither of which are
vendible Commodities Abroad."

## Appeals to Prejudices

There are relatively few direct appeals to the prejudices
of the reader, but such is not surprising when one recalls
that the peculiar nature of the proposal is such that the interests of both Ireland and England are brought together
and that the adverse side of the argument is represented only
by the *Craftsman*.

Perhaps it is only accidental, but it is nevertheless interesting to note that the two appeals to religious prejudices are
also neatly balanced: there is one directed against Roman
Catholics and one against the Anglicans. In urging the financial
advantage of this commerce, the projector points out that
if both the French and Spanish kings buy this export and
then become involved in a war with each other, both monarchs will require great numbers of Irishmen. Since only
Roman Catholics sell themselves to these monarchs, "how
soon would those Recruits be destroyed, then what a Number
of Friends would the Pretender lose, and what a Number of
Popish Enemies all true Protestants get rid of."

Appealing to the non-conformists' prejudice against the Establishment, the author states,

AS to the Civil and Ecclesiastical Administration, which I have not yet fully considered, I can say little; only with Regard to the latter, it is plain, that the Article of paying Tythe for supporting speculative Opinions in Religion, which is so insupportable a Burthen to all true Protestants, and to most Churchmen, will be very much lessened by this Expedient; because dry Cattle pay nothing to the spiritual Hireling, any more than Imported Corn. . . .

## CONCLUSIONS

The basic ironic pose of the essay is established by the ethical proof, with the projector's clear Anglo-Irish sympathies, his double patriotic motive for offering the proposal, and his demonstration of his competency as an historian, thinker, and economic projector. The ethical proof goes far in establishing the ironic norm, but this norm is further indicated by the intricate patterns of diminution and amplification. It is only by the reader's threading his way through these devices that he can deduce the value-system which informs them and through which they must therefore be understood. There are, of course, other ways for an ironist to indicate the ironic norm. The point here is that Swift chose to use the devices of classical rhetoric.

"The Answer to the *Craftsman*" can quite accurately be termed a sequel to "A Modest Proposal," for it is an ironical proposal which presents yet another method for benefiting Ireland by selling Irish flesh. The major difference in the content of the proposals is that whereas the earlier proposal, negatively, could in no way "disoblige *England*," the present one will, positively, render England "a prodigious Gainer." Here Swift makes the fullest use of the letter of the law, emphasizing as he does the complete "legality" of his proposal. In paragraph three the author cites the specific acts of Parliament which control and allow such commerce. In the next paragraph he calls the reader's attention to the legality of the scheme: "Our truest and best Ally the most Christian King hath obtained his Majesty's Licence, pursuant to Law, to export from here . . . ." And in paragraph thirteen the author, in giving a brief historical sketch of the conquest of Ireland, emphasizes the justness (i.e., the legality) of England's economic demands upon Ireland. In addition to these specific passages, the author repeatedly justifies his scheme upon the basis that England will indeed be required to furnish all manufactured articles, pursuant to the old relationship established by the Irish princes and Prince Henry II.

The similarities being so great between these two essays, one might naturally expect a great degree of similarities in rhetorical method. The similarity exists, but not to such a degree as might at first be expected. In the first proposal Swift has used an elaborate combination of major and minor rhetorical devices in an intricate pattern. In the second proposal he has used only a few of the more basic devices: ethical proof, diminution, and amplification. Perhaps this fact in a large measure accounts for the differing degrees of excellence between the two essays. "A Modest Proposal" is perfect; "The Answer to the *Craftsman*" is good. The second reason for such a judgment is the variation of intensity between the two. Although the second essay has a tone of immediacy and urgency, it does not so often strike fire, and its ironic rhetoric is not so consistently intensive and extensive. Such statements, however, do not detract from "The Answer to the *Craftsman*," for in its less ambitious way and in its smaller scale it can stand quite proudly with its more famous predecessor. It is the excellent use of rhetoric in the creation and sustaining of the irony in this essay which admits it to favourable comparison with "A Modest Proposal" and which allows it justly to be a companion piece.

## CHAPTER VI

# Recurring Rhetorical Patterns

THE many devices of classical rhetoric which Swift employed do not all contribute with the same force to the creation of the irony of these essays. From the several degrees of pertinence which these devices have to the creation of the irony, it is possible to distinguish three significant groups: those which actually create the irony and thus are integral to its very existence (ethical proof, amplification, diminution, and refining); those which, although not integral, contribute almost as substantially as does the first group (appeal to authority, elimination, argument from parallel example, and argument from a wealth of sources); and those which help sustain the irony but which do not actually create it (litotes, direct emotional appeal, interrogation, rhetorical question, personification, climax, anti-climax, and accumulation).

Keeping constantly in mind that it is the total complex of these devices and their interactions on each other which give the full texture to the irony of these essays, one may safely and profitably examine the several actions of the individual devices and the several degrees to which Swift employs them in the creation of the ironies.

## MAJOR RHETORICAL DEVICES

Aristotle has stated that all artificial proof is of three kinds: the ethical, the argumentative, and the emotional. His equating these three would suggest that each bears equal importance in the burden of proof. Of course, to theorize mathematically on this matter is valueless, but one can use Aristotle's tripartite division to show how heavily Swift valued the ethical proof as the basic, sustaining, and unifying device of classical rhetoric in the creation of the irony of these essays.

Irony requires a pose, which sets distance between the reader and the ironic situation and which, when perceived by the reader, gives him the point of view from which he is to understand the irony. Some authors become ironists personally in their writing; others operate through a dramatic "I." Swift has gone far beyond either method by using the ethical proof of classical rhetoric and creating a rather fully developed character to be the "author" of his ironic inversions. Doing so has therefore given Swift a more powerful irony than the other methods could have, for as degree of irony is directly proportionate to the rhetorical distance set up between the reader and the thing satirized, Swift's working through a separate character creates a greater distance than do the other two methods.[1] The use of this device accounts substantially for the frequently terrifying power of Swift's ironies, a power so great that Swift dwarfs every other ironist in our language.

A further advantage that Swift gains through his use of this device is that every sentence of each essay has a reality of its own and is never vitiated into generality, because an individual, the personalized "author," has written it and has stamped upon it his own point of view and mode and tone of expression. The defender of Lord Carteret is, for example, an extremely moderate Whig in defence of another moderate Whig; and, although he and the projector of the modest proposal have several characteristics which are similar (conservatism, reasonableness, moderation), they differ because the defender is not also an economic mathematician and a projector. Swift has his projector write a second proposal, in answer to the *Craftsman*; however, new facets of the projector's personality emerge in the second essay because the projector has been challenged and vexed by Mr. D'Anvers, the author of the *Craftsman* article, who has been "pleased, without a Call, officiously and maliciously to interpose with very frivolous Arguments." Throughout the second essay, therefore, the projector writes in an aggressive and truculent tone which is lacking in the first proposal.

Swift establishes the ethical proof by having his author reflect his reasonableness, his competence (sometimes through acute historical knowledge, usually through elaborate mathe-

matical proofs), his mental astuteness, his conservative esti-
mates and evaluations, and his love of country (the highest
of all motives for orators). In addition to establishing these
qualities, Swift also employs two rhetorical devices in creating the ethical proof: deference and concession, both of which
contribute to the illusion of reasonableness. Concession is
most elaborately used in the defence of Lord Carteret,
where it is made the informing principle of the whole
essay. The broad movement of the essay is the author's conceding point after point (over twenty-eight separate ones)
until at the very end of the essay he is able to reverse the flow
of concessions with a powerful litotes. The situation at the
end of this essay is typical of Swift's rhetorical method: the
amassing of several rhetorical devices operating in close combination. Here the litotes, coupled with accumulation and
turning the charge, overbalances the flow of concession,
which is already in operation to contribute to the ethical
proof. All of these "authors" are artistically realized
characters unlike each other and unlike Swift himself. One
must seek the real Swift as rhetorician in such works as his
sermons and the *Four Last Years of the Queen*, where he
is using in his own person many of the same devices of classical rhetoric he employs for ironical purposes in these essays.

Swift first used a *persona* in *A Tale of a Tub*, written, of
course, by the "modern author," who generally confused most
of Swift's contemporaries, including, it is said, the Queen.
One might object that a writer's creation of a character to
be his spokesman is neither peculiar to classical rhetoric nor
to any particular period of our literature. Gulliver, who is
only remotely related laterally to these "authors," is primarily
the narrator-hero of a satiric travel novel, and as such is
not clearly related to classical rhetoric. However, the authors
of these essays are not dramatic characters, who move in a
narrative; they are orators delivering polemic orations for or
against something. Each argues in the forum; each uses a
wealth of other devices of classical rhetoric, the projector
of the modest proposal going so far as to cast his whole essay
into the form of a classical oration. Thus, if the ethical proof
were an isolated rhetorical device which Swift employed in
these essays, one could simply suggest that it is related to

classical rhetoric; but Swift has amassed many other devices of classical rhetoric to build his ironies. This complex combination of a large number of these devices makes these essays orations and makes these *personae* serve as ethical proof and not merely as the author's spokesmen.

Swift was not, however, slavish in using his "authors." They are simply a *modus operandi* through which he works, for, as I have shown, Swift sometimes remains silently behind his author and at other times steps forward to take matters into his own hands. Swift's constantly varying the degree of irony by the degree of his own presence adds fascinating dimension to his ironic satire and keeps the ethical proof from ever becoming a wooden or cumbersome device.

Although the ethical proof is a major contributor to the establishing of the ironic norm, Swift is not content to rely upon a single device. In all of these essays he reinforces and elucidates the ironic norm through deftly controlled amplification and diminution.

In "A Modest Proposal" Swift diminishes Irish parents to "Breeders" and children to animals fit for food. He varies the animal, food, and normal terms, inserting first one and then another term to the reader until the ironic norm is fixed, and within the context of the ironic inversion Swift achieves the illusion that year-old Irish babies are cattle. He carries the device a step beyond the ancients when he redoubles the diminution by first rendering the children as cattle and then the cattle as fine foods for "Gentlemen of Taste and Pleasure." A salient characteristic of Swift's use of classical rhetoric is the multiplicity of it: not only does he interlock different devices to create or sustain the irony; he also proliferates a single device. The diminution in "A Modest Proposal" is a case in point. Swift diminishes the parents *in order to* diminish the children, and by implication he diminishes the Irish and Anglo-Irish who will eat this new food. The separate threads of the diminution are thus woven together, and this device, already stemming directly from the ethical proof, is then interlocked with the refining of the gentlemen of pleasure, who first are seen only as the persons to whom this food will be offered for sale, later as the consumers of this new food, and finally as the cause of the whole situation in Ireland which has brought about the need for the proposal in the first place.

In the Christianity essay Swift further indicates the ironic norm by diminishing the ministers and the old classical education and by amplifying the profound freethinkers, the new education, and the polite world. In this essay the personality of the "author," being somewhat befuddled, is not a sufficient vehicle for Swift's communicating the ironic norm. Amplification and diminution are needed to make it clear. Diminution and amplification are major creators of the irony because both devices must be derived from a value-system and judgment which they in turn reflect, and in the ironical inversions the "author's" point of view is the ironic norm. This clinical separation of these three devices is misleading, for, after all, the amplification and diminution spring from the mouth of the pleader. Swift never advances singly; he moves his whole rhetorical army forward at once.

In the defence of Lord Carteret, Swift again employs amplification and diminution to help create the ironic norm. The Whig "author" amplifies both himself and Lord Carteret as moderate, sensible Whigs and diminishes the Whig "Zealots" who have attacked Lord Carteret, ultimately rendering *them* as the eccentric, unorthodox extremists. From this unique position the author is then able to enrich the diminution by hurling at his opponents all of the offensive epithets usually reserved for Tories. Concurrent with this diminution is that of classical education. Thus, although the author associates himself with one line of the diminution, being a good "modern," he does not associate himself with the diminution of classicism.

Of all the complex amplification-diminution in these essays, that of "The Answer to the *Craftsman*" is the most complex. Swift argues himself into the position that through exporting Irish flesh to the French armies and making Ireland a "new Arcadia," the best interests of both Ireland and England will be served. From this position Swift diminishes some of the Irish to the animal term (those who are to be exported to France) and amplifies the remaining Irish Arcadians while simultaneously amplifying the English. Superimposed upon this network of devices is Swift's burlesque of the Arcadianism.

In addition to the major contribution which amplification

and diminution make to the creation of the irony by indicating the ironic norm of these essays, these two devices, being structurally important and being verbal, contribute also to the thematic unity of the essays. The constant weaving in and out of the vocabulary of amplification and diminution binds the paragraphs together.

## COMPLEMENTARY RHETORICAL DEVICES

Complementing the devices just discussed are others which function as shoring agents: as the ethical proof, amplification, diminution, and refining are creating the irony, these other devices are intimately involved in supporting, sustaining, and expanding the irony. They are elimination, argument from a wealth of material, parallel example, and appeal to authority.

Swift frequently joins argument by elimination to argument from a wealth of material. Adroitly excluding all other possibilities as inoperable or unsound suggests the "rightness" of his own proposal, and by coupling this device with wealth of material he gives the impression that he has chosen as many arguments as he has space to use. When in "A Modest Proposal" Swift states, "MANY other Advantages might be enumerated . . . . But this, and many Others, I omit; being studious of Brevity . . . ," he indicates the wealth of possible arguments and examples which he might draw upon.

Elimination does not occur in the Christianity essay, abundance of arguments and materials being dominant and sufficient. Otherwise, elimination and argument from wealth of material are constants in these essays. In the defence of Lord Carteret, Swift only apparently does not use elimination. There he creates the illusion of debating from a strong position by actually discussing at length all the cases (only four) cited in the attacks upon Lord Carteret. Thus his defence seems exhaustive, but near the end of the essay, argument from a wealth of sources and elimination are brought into play in combination when the author states that he has avoided even mentioning the large number of appointments of real Tories in England and that he has dealt only with the appointments of alleged Tories in Ireland. Thus he has at once eliminated his strongest arguments from English Tories and has indicated the wealth of real material which would further exonerate Lord Carteret. Except for this detail in this essay Swift manages to cast over these essays the illusion that he is dealing only with salient material at the heart of the question and that many more proofs can be found by whoever cares to. Such implications contribute to the irony by implying that the ironic norm does not rest simply on the briefly stated material within the essay but that the world *outside* the inversion will also support the ironic norm.

The appeal to parallel example offers the same kind of buttressing: "BUT let me suppose a very possible Case." "Suppose, for Argument Sake, that the *Tories* favoured *Margarita*, the *Whigs* Mrs. *Tofts*, and the *Trimmers Valentini*. . . ." This drawing upon real or ostensibly real events outside of the ironic world further supports the ironic norm, casting over it the aura of "rightness."

Closely allied to this "outside witnessing" is the appeal to authority. To appeal to that "grave Author" Rabelais, to an "eminent Physician, who is well versed in such profound Speculations," to the bishops of Ireland, lends plausibility (and therefore acceptability) to the irony by enlisting great names and personages as authorities for what is being said. Swift, however, follows Aristotle and pushes such appeals far beyond individuals to include the "Wisdom of the Nation," proverbs, Toland and the mass of freethinkers, "all Mankind." Through this device Swift succeeds in involving the whole society in the ironic norm, and it is this fact which contributes heavily to the universality of Swift's satire and makes it more far-reaching than the immediate subjects of the essays would seem to indicate. And it is this fact which helps answer the question, How can a topical satiric essay written to attack a specific English policy in Ireland in the early decades of the eighteenth century continue to have abiding interest and application?

Swift's use of appeal to authority is extensive in all of the essays; and, given the ironic pose, the authorities function in the classical manner. Only in the defence of Lord Carteret does Swift move beyond classical usage of this device. There he attacks the shoddy sources of the criticism against Lord Carteret by imitating the opponents' appeal to the authority of general rumor and spies. Thus Swift undercuts with a telling irony the very authorities which he purports to be calling forth.

### SUPPLEMENTARY RHETORICAL DEVICES

The devices discussed thus far actually create the ironies of these essays. The remaining devices—climax, anticlimax, litotes, direct emotional appeal, ocular demonstration, interrogation, rhetorical question, parenthesis, and personification—help sustain the irony, but they do not create it. In addition to their giving a classical texture to the essays (and thereby lending them a further weight of authority of the ancient and traditional), four of these (litotes, parenthesis, interrogation, rhetorical question) are modes of expression and are thus devices through which the major devices operate—for example, the introduction of an amplification or an authority into a parenthesis or by means of a litotes.

Litotes serves a variety of functions. The casual verbal ironies lend an air of urbanity to the author's tone, a quality to which they all pretend. Litotes is used to maintain the thin veil of surface inversion in "A Modest Proposal" when the author almost breaks through with the simple truth: the proposer concedes that this food "will be somewhat dear" and that the practice of selling the babies might be censured by some "scrupulous People," "(although indeed very unjustly) as a little bordering upon Cruelty. . . ." The most crucial use to which Swift puts litotes occurs in his defence of Lord Carteret, in which, after three-quarters of the essay has been spent conceding the "Faults" of that nobleman, the author reckons the Tory and Whig balances of remunerations from employments and concludes with an enormous Whig balance and a slight Tory one: ". . . So, I do not find how his Excellency can be justly censured for favouring none [but Tories] . . . . When by a fair State of the Account; the Ballance, I conceive, *seems to lie* on the other Side." Here the litotes bears the whole burden of overbalancing the long flow of concessions.

Climax, anticlimax, and accumulation function in two major ways in these essays. They are used specifically in individual sentences, and they are used as the basis of the general arrangement and movement of some of the essays. The author of the modest proposal combines accumulation and anti-climax in the final paragraph when he disclaims any personal motive for writing. He has "no other Motive than the *publick Good of my Country, by advancing our Trade, providing for Infants, relieving the Poor, and giving some Pleasure to the Rich.*" Accumulation thus summarizes the major points raised in the essay, and the anticlimax occurs when Swift places the pleasures of the rich in final position. But this same paragraph contains a good example of the broader kind of anti-climax. The whole disclaimer and the statement that the pro-jector's wife is past childbearing serve to end the essay on a minor note, a slight off-hand undercutting. This general rhythm of rising climactically only to be finally undercut occurs in all of the essays as well as in individual sentences and paragraphs. The arguments against abolishing Christianity roll forth in amazing waves, culminating in the accumulation of the four concisely and rapidly stated reasons for the reten-tion of Christianity, all of which is slyly undercut in the final paragraph, where the author states that the abolition might cause the stock of the East India Company to fall one per cent. "And, since that is Fifty Times more than ever the Wisdom of our Age thought fit to venture for the *Preser-vation* of Christianity, there is no Reason we should be at so great a Loss, meerly for the Sake of *destroying* it." This same general movement informs the defence of Lord Carteret, which ends with the litotes just discussed. The thrill of this irony of anticlimax is almost as great at the end of single sentences as it is at the end of whole essays. One recalls the modest pro-poser's statement that a child will "be very good Boiled on the fourth Day, especially in *Winter.*"

Swift uses direct appeal to the emotions to gain pity for his subject (as in the ocular demonstration which opens "A Modest Proposal"), to play upon his reader's fears of the Pretender and the Roman Church, and to indicate for the ethical proof that these fears are also the author's prejudices.

Swift uses interrogation to level specific questions at his opponents and in the more loosely rhetorical method of posing questions which, if left purely rhetorical, might not have their answers properly controlled. However, the rhetorical question as such is abundantly used in all of the essays. Swift frequently uses it to imply a tone of exasperation with his opponents, and in his defence of Christianity he uses it to vary the otherwise uninterrupted flow of formal "argument" and to indicate that many of his opponents' objections are not worthy of reply and deserve merely to be parried by a counter question.

Personification is used only once in all of the essays: its use in the Christianity essay therefore gives it the startling power of uniqueness when that goddess, the Spirit of Opposition, springs to life in that essay: ". . . there is one darling Inclination of a Mankind, which usually affects to be a Retainer to Religion, although she be neither its Parent, its Godmother, or its Friend; I mean the Spirit of Opposition, that lived long before Christianity, and can easily subsist without it."

These supplementary devices alone could probably never create a good, sustained ironic inversion; but, coupled as they are with the major rhetorical devices of these essays, they make a major contribution to the total rhetorical texture and to the irony through their own qualities and through the sheer mass and complexity with which Swift has used them.

### PERORATION

No one in his century had as little confidence in or respect for the reasoning powers of man or for his ability really to know, as Swift had. Having come of age with the New Philosophy, he rejected both scholasticism and the new science and with a medieval faith held firm to Christian orthodoxy. Since he believed he could not depend upon man's using his capacity to reason, it is not surprising that Swift quite naturally turned to the persuasive power of ancient rhetoric to convince man of his sins and follies and to indicate right action—quite naturally, because Swift's whole grammar school and university training was in this rhetoric. Swift used it both consciously as an Art of Rhetoric and by second nature. How consciously is a moot question. Because these essays are occasional, Swift must have had the occasion and the practical application of ironic rhetoric uppermost in mind. However, considering the high degree of excellence of all of these essays it is difficult to believe that subject matter took precedence over method at the time of composition. The answer is, of course, a secret of genius, upon which speculation becomes idle. Indicating so fully Swift's application of the rules of the art of rhetoric might tend to imply that Swift was hidebound to these rules; but, as I have indicated earlier, such is not the case. His dexterity within the rules and his not hesitating to burst beyond the bounds of rules when he cares to, belie the impression.

What these essays might have been without their firm structure of classical rhetoric creating the irony buttressed by more classical rhetoric expanding and sustaining the irony cannot be contemplated. They could not be what they are without this rhetoric, and an exploration and examination of the classical rhetoric in these essays yields yet another way in which to understand the method and to praise the work of the greatest prose ironist in our language. It also gives yet another reason for wishing that Swift had vouchsafed the world more of his grave formal lies.

# Notes

## CHAPTER I

[1]An examination of the curricula of the two schools will amply demonstrate this statement. For an approximate description of the kind of instruction offered at Kilkenny, "The Eton of Ireland," see that of the English schools upon which it was modeled, as described in Foster Watson, *The Old Grammar Schools* (Cambridge: The University Press, 1916), in which Professor Watson depends heavily upon John Brinsley's *Ludus Literarius, or the Grammar School* (1st ed. 1612) and Hoole's *New Discovery of the Old Art of Teaching School*, which, although not published until 1660, incorporates Brinsley's account and which is based upon experience prior to the Puritan Revolution. For the best descriptions of the thoroughly rhetorical training offered at Trinity when Swift was there, see John William Stubbs, *The History of the University of Dublin from Its Foundation to the End of the 18th Century* ("Dublin University Series"; Dublin: 1890) and the following articles published in *Hermathena*: R. B. McDowell and D. A. Webb, "Courses and Teaching in Trinity College, Dublin, during the First 200 Years," LXIX (May, 1947) and E. J. Furlong, "The Study of Logic in Trinity College, Dublin," LX (Nov., 1942).

[2]Cf. Quintilian *Institutio Oratoria* III. vii. 1-18. for the rhetorical devices of encomia which Swift makes use of here, as well as for those which he attacks in the panegyric to Lord Somers.

[3]Swift is not a major figure in the great 17th-century debate on style, for by the end of that century, the proponents of the Plain Style were in the ascendance over proponents of the use of elaborate figures in expository writing. See W. Frazer Mitchell, *English Pulpit Oratory from Andrewes to Tillotson* (London: Society for Promoting Christian Knowledge, 1932) for a background study of the elaborate style which was later to be attacked on grounds that vague figures of speech further obscure cloudy reasoning; Harold Fisch, "The Puritans and the Reform of Prose-Style," *ELH*, XIX (Dec., 1952), pp. 229-48, for the thesis that the debate was not simply between Puritan and Anglican preachers but was among preachers in general without regard to denominational lines; Richard F. Jones, "The Attack on Pulpit Eloquence in the Restoration," *JEGP*, XXX (1931), pp. 188-227, for the thesis that the debate was entirely scientific in origin, beginning with Bacon and culminating in the efforts of the Royal Society. The truth lies, it seems to me, in the fact that no single group was responsible for the shift toward the Plain Style. The members of the Royal Society did their share, the Ramists did theirs, and the great prose writers such as Dryden, Cowley (in his later work), and Swift (a bit later) did theirs. Swift, writing after the debate had substantially been settled, reflects the opinion of his time and reinforces it rather than leads it.

[4]Harold D. Kelling, "Reason in Madness: *A Tale of a Tub*," *PMLA*, LXIX (March, 1954), pp. 198-222.

[5]Swift cites *omniscience, omnipresence, ubiquity, attribute, beatific vision, entity* as words to be avoided. Also, he recommends that difficult passages

149

from Scriptures, especially St. Paul, should be paraphrased into simpler language rather than quoted.

⁶For Swift's vigorous running comments on style, see his marginalia on Burnet's *History of His Own Times*, where Swift indicates his extreme displeasure at what he considers to be Bishop Burnet's hollow eloquence and "wrong arguing," printed in the Temple Scott edition of Swift's *Works*, X, 327-68. Somewhat more temperate comments on eloquence appear in this same volume (pp. 291-323) in Swift's marginalia on Clarendon's *History of the Rebellion*.

⁷Swift's distinction between the oratorical mission of Demosthenes and Cicero and that of a Christian minister can be seen to be a justification for Swift's own elaborate use of rhetoric in the heat of political pamphlet warfare; his role as a political writer corresponds to that of the ancient orator.

⁸A good example is Swift's sermon "Upon Sleeping in Church," which also contains further comments on rhetoric in sermons.

## CHAPTER II

¹Aristole divides all proof into two areas: inartificial (the facts which exist) and artificial (the use made of the facts through the art of rhetoric). He divides artificial proof into three kinds: ethical, emotional, and logical. The ethical proof stems from the moral character of the pleader himself (*Rhet.* I.ii.3). Quintilian agrees: although the pleader "may be modest and say little about himself, yet if he is believed to be a good man, this consideration will exercise the strongest influence at every point in the case. For thus he will have the good fortune to give the impression not so much that he is a zealous advocate as that he is an absolutely reliable witness. It is therefore pre-eminently desirable that he should be believed to have undertaken the case out of a sense of duty, by a sense of patriotism or at any rate some serious moral consideration" (*Instit.* IV.i.7.). The texts I have used are those of the Loeb Classical Library. *The Art of Rhetoric*, Tr. John Henry Freeze (London: William Heinemann, Ltd., 1947) and *Institutio Oratoria*, Tr. H. E. Butler( London, 1953).

²A pleader must reflect self-confidence in himself and in his own proposals if he expects his audience to be convinced. The classical rhetoricians agree that the best delivery is that in which the pleader either participates in or seems to participate in the emotions and convictions which he is displaying.

³Quintilian *Instit.* VI.ii.26.: "The prime essential for stirring the emotions of others is, in my opinion, first to feel these emotions oneself." See also Cicero *De Oratore* II.xlv.189.

⁴Decreasing the population of Ireland would, as the projector views the problem, improve the situation by lessening the number of people to be fed and otherwise maintained. But, the projector continues, this proposal is calculated "*for this one individual Kingdom of* IRELAND, *and for no other that ever was, is, or I think ever can be upon Earth.*" Landa points out that an argument which recurs in Swift's Irish tracts is that, because the situation in Ireland is so pitifully unique, the best maxims on government and economics cannot operate there. Swift seems to have accepted the mercantile concept that the people are the wealth of a nation and that prosperity is dependent upon a constantly increasing population. (See Louis A. Landa, "*A Modest Proposal* and Populousness," *MP*, XL (Nov., 1942), pp. 161-70.) The projector's statement is an ironical inversion of the maxim. Also, of course, Swift is making use of the maxim by rendering it literal:

in "A Modest Proposal" the infants are literally to be the wealth of the nation.

[5]Swift seems here to be satirizing the economic projectors, whose pamphlets abound in mazes of mathematics. See George Wittkowsky, "Swift's 'Modest Proposal'; the Biography of an Early Georgian Pamphlet," *Journal of the History of Ideas*, IV (Jan., 1943), pp. 75-104.

[6]I have here used the name *concession* for this device. Quintilian discusses concession, confession, and agreement as allied figures "which have a strong family resemblance." All three are used to concede points "that can do our case no harm." The act of concession implies a strong, confident position. (*Instit.* IX.ii.51-52.).

[7]Ricardo Quintana, *The Mind and Art of Jonathan Swift* (Oxford: The University Press, 1936), p. 43. Several of the examples of diminution partake also of comparison; but, since diminution is the broader term for this particular context, all those examples of comparison will be considered in this section.

[8]In addition to this terminology's function in the animal diminution, it also satirizes the economic projector who is wont to deal with people as if they were only statistics, or as if they were cattle.

[9]The projector states, "I have reckoned upon a Medium, that a Child just born will weigh Twelve Pounds. . . ." The very grossness of the figure *12* suggests that it is a part of the animal diminution and is to be taken as an inhuman size for an *average* child at birth (for an average of 12 pounds requires some weights to be at least as high as 16 pounds). We should not, however, be too quick to apply mid-twentieth-century obstetrical standards to this figure. Only unavailable medical case histories of early 18th-century Ireland could prove the point. It is always possible that Swift simply did not know about such things, but if this be the case, it is the only instance in the whole essay which he has not investigated to the minutest detail.

[10]*Rhetorica ad Herennium*, tr. Harry Caplan (Loeb Classical Library; London: William Heinemann, Ltd., 1954), IV.xlii.54.

[11]Martin Price, *Swift's Rhetorical Art: A Study in Structure and Meaning* (New Haven: Yale University Press, 1953), pp. 27-31.

[12]Aristotle *Rhet.* II.xxiii.12. See also Quintilian *Instit.* V.xi.36-37.

[13]Quintana suggests that Swift was strongly Anglo-Irish instead of Irish (Quintana, *op. cit.*, pp. 246-47). Murry believes that Swift's motives are too unclear or mixed for us to determine. John Middleton Murry, *Jonathan Swift: A Critical Biography* (London: Jonathan Cape, 1954), p. 359. Davis, in his Introduction to Vol. X of his edition of *The Drapier Letters* calls attention to the fact that the Drapier addressed himself to the "whole State of Ireland" (p. xxxi). Carl Van Doren suggests that Swift's strong pro-Anglo-Irish sentiment gradually gave way to a pan-Irish sympathy by the end of the Wood campaign. Van Doren cites Swift's own comment in a letter to Pope: "I do profess without affectation, that your kind opinion of me as a patriot, since you call it so, is what I do not deserve; because what I do is owing to perfect rage and resentment, and the mortifying sight of slavery, folly, and baseness about me, among which I am forced to live." Carl Van Doren, *Swift* (New York: The Viking Press, 1930), pp. 170-71. Swift himself could probably not have determined whether his vexation against English injustice to Ireland was greater or less than his disgust at Irish apathy which accepted English policies.

[14]*Ad Herennium* LV.

[15]See Swift's "A Short View of the State of Ireland" for a description of the plight of the agricultural worker and of the depleted condition of many of the old plantations.

[16]In general in this essay italics are used for emphasis and might therefore be construed as a hint concerning that part of oratory called delivery. However, the well-known problems of Swift and his printers on such textual matters render only dubious authenticity to any particular italics. We cannot know for sure whether some are Swift's or his printer's.

## CHAPTER III

[1]Jonathan Swift, *Bickerstaff Papers and Pamphlets on the Church*, ed. Herbert Davis (Oxford: Basil Blackwell, 1957), p. xvii.

[2]The author of *Ad Herennium* discusses a "Figure of Thought" which he calls Frankness of Speech (*oratio libera*). He states that "It is Frankness of Speech when, talking before those to whom we owe reverence or fear, we yet exercise our right to speak out, because we seem justified in reprehending them, or persons dear to them, for some fault" (IV.xxxvi.). Quintilian denies that this is a figure (*Instit.* IX.ii.27. and IX.iii.99.).

[3]See *Examiner's* No. 13, 15, 25, and especially 33.

[4]*NED*, Vol. VII, Pt. II, p. 496: In the extended use of the word *parson* to name any beneficed clergyman, the word is only colloquial and, except in rural use, is usually "more or less depreciatory and dyslogistic."

[5]The *NED* cites Jonson (1616) as first use of *projector* invidiously (Vol. VII, Pt. II, p. 1445). The verb *to undertake* meaning to entrap, to take by craft, was obsolete by the 16th century; however, an undertaker in 16th and 17th Ireland was an Englishman who undertook to hold crown lands. This definition continued as late as 1888. An undertaker in the reigns of Charles Martyr and Charles II was a man who undertook to control Parliament, especially in the granting of royal supplies. (*NED*, Vol. X, Pt. I, p. 151). Goldsmith (1774) is the earliest citation for the pejorative use of *expedient*, beyond the connotation that an innovation is a "novelty." (*NED*, Vol. V, Pt. I, p. 496).

[6]Quintilian states that the simplest form of amplification (*amplificandi*) is to be found in the actual word employed to describe a thing. See *Instit.* VIII, iv. for Quintilian's complete discussion of this device. He first states that amplification means only an intensification through choice of word and that an idea can thus be intensified either by the use of the better or best word or by the use of the worse or worst word. In his discussion he tends to use *amplification* to name the use of the better word and *attenuation* (*minuendi*) to name the use of the worse word. (I have used *diminution* to name this device.) Quintilian states, "I am not a stickler for exact terminology, provided the sense is clear to any serious student."

[7]William B. Ewald (in *The Masks of Jonathan Swift* [Cambridge: Harvard University Press, 1954], p. 49) states, "Perhaps he neglects his pose when the author refers to the 'trumpery' of the deist writers, because he later praises their 'wonderful productions of wit'; when he speaks of the 'scrofulous, consumptive' offspring of 'our men of wit and pleasure,' because he later includes some of them among the 'wise reformers' opposed to Christianity." Ewald concludes that these are only minor flaws. Quintana has suggested that the apparent inconsistency results from the principle of composition through multiple voices: the speaker presents a dialogue among his "various selves." (Ricardo Quintana, "Situational Satire: a Com-

mentary on the Method of Swift," in *Studies in Literature of the Augustan Age*, ed. Richard C. Boys [Ann Arbor, 1952], pp. 259-65, reprinted from the *University of Toronto Quarterly*, XVII [1948], 130-206).
[8]See *Examiner* No. 31 for a genealogy of Party and No. 30 for a genealogy of Merit.

## CHAPTER IV

[1]For a fuller characterization of Carteret and his life in Dublin, see Basil Williams, *Carteret and Newcastle: a Contrast in Contemporaries* (Cambridge: the University Press, 1943), Chapter V, "Carteret in Dublin and in Private Life," pp. 70-92.
[2]*The Correspondence of Jonathan Swift, D. D.*, ed. F. Elrington Ball (London: George Bell and Sons, Ltd., 1910-1914), IV, 179.
[3]See Henry Knight Miller, "The Paradoxical Encomium with Special Reference to Its Vogue in England, 1600-1800," *MP*, LIII (Feb., 1956, pp.145-78, for a good (although not in all points complete) discussion of the paradoxical encomium. A paradoxical encomium is positive praise of an unworthy subject; and, although Swift's "Vindication" is not technically in this classical genre, its ironic praise makes it sufficiently akin to the classical paradoxical encomium for one to profit from a knowledge of this genre when he reads Swift's essay.
[4]Pistorides is Richard Tighe, who informed on Dr. Sheridan when the latter preached at Cork.
[5]The phrase applied to the Whigs to name the Tory administration during the last four years of the reign of Queen Anne. This was the Harley-St. John ministry, in which Swift was intimately involved.
[6]A note in the original edition identifies Madame Violante as a famous Italian rope-dancer.
[7]Hutcheson had appeared in the Irish House of Commons in support of a Sergeant Bettesworts, who had appealed to that body for defense against a lampoon written by Swift. Subsequent to the writing of the present essay, it was Hutcheson who signed the order committing Swift's publisher Faulkner to prison for publishing a pamphlet which, although not written by Swift, was approved by Swift.
[8]Traulus was Joshua, Lord Allen, who was thought by his contemporaries to suffer from some kind of madness. Dean Swift prided himself on his never attacking a fool unless that fool set himself up for a wit. See his lampooning of Allen in his poem "Traulus" and his "Advertisement by Dr. Swift, in his Defence against Joshua, Lord Allen," in both of which Swift attacks Lord Allen for his perfidy and simultaneous fawning over the Dean.

## CHAPTER V

[1]The *Craftsman* was an anti-Walpole periodical founded by Pulteney after his break with Walpole. Its mission was to aid in the organization of a coalition of Tories and disaffected Whigs. Bolingbroke was its famous "Occasional Writer," and Temple Scott states that Walpole, not being fooled by the Grub Street fiction "Caleb D'Anvers," immediately recognized the hand of Bolingbroke, as is indicated by the strong reply Walpole wrote in answer to the first number of the Occasional Writer. Temple Scott edition of Swift's *Works*, VII, 219, n. 1.
[2]Acts of the English Parliament in 1665 and 1680 completely ruined the Irish cattle trade. The good grazing land was then used to raise sheep, and soon a flourishing industry developed. In 1699 the woolen industry

was crippled by an Act of Parliament prohibiting the export of wool to any country except England and Wales. The linen industry was encouraged in order to displace the woolen industry; however, this was no immediate remedy because the skills involved are so different as to render difficult a woolen craftsman's adjusting to the new trade. Also, the linen industry was dominated by Scotsmen in the northern counties and was not immediately available to Irishmen.

[3]Swift also implies that the new Arcadia will be the Zion prophesied by Micah. Cf. the King James Version of Micah 4:10: "But they shall sit every man under his vine and under his fig tree; and none shall make them afraid; for the mouth of the Lord of hosts hath spoken it."

[4]Although these figures are somewhat exaggerated for satiric purpose, they are not so exaggerated as might at first appear. W. E. H. Lecky in his *A History of Ireland in the Eighteenth Century* (5 Vols. New York: D. Appleton & Co., 1893) states that during the Cromwellian period 30 to 40 thousand Irishmen went into foreign military service (I, 104). Lecky quotes the chaplain of the Irish Brigade of the French Army as follows: "The Abbé MacGeoghegan . . . makes this extraordinary assertion: 'Par les calcels et les recherches faites au bureau de la guerre on a trouvé qu'il y avait eu depuis l'arrivée des troupes Irlandoises en France, en 1691, jusqu'en 1745, que se donna la bataille de Fontenoy, plus de 450,000 Irlandois morts au service de France.' [It was a unit made up mainly of Irish troops which finally broke the English column at Fontenoy.] (*Hist. d'Irlande*, iii, 745). This statement is to me perfectly incredible, but Newenham, in his valuable work *On the Population of Ireland* says 'Upon the whole, I am inclined to think that we are not sufficiently warranted in considering the Abbé MacGeoghegan's statement as an exaggeration.' (p. 63); and O'Callaghan, in his *Hist. of the Irish Brigade in the Service of France*, cites two MS. authorities, professedly based on researches made in the French War Office, which place the number even higher" (I, 248.).

## CHAPTER VI

[1]See David Worcester, *The Art of Satire* (Cambridge: Harvard University Press, 1940), *passim* and especially pp. 29-32.

# Glossary

[Note: The classical rhetorical terms and principles are explained in the text or footnotes as the need occurs, but are seldom repeated. They are collected here for convenient reference.]

*Accumulation*: the clustering of ideas or arguments to gain added power, especially when the elements singly have little power.

*Amplification*: using the better word or implying the better motive to name or evaluate an act or person.

*Anticlimax*: reversing a series by placing a lesser word or idea in the final position.

*Appeal to Authority*: calling for corroboration a specific person, the speaker's eye-witness testimony, or the opinion of the majority (including proverbs, which contain the general wisdom of the majority).

*Argument from parallel example*: arguing from an example which actually or ostensibly parallels the situation being debated — the example usually being drawn from history, literature, fable, or current events.

*Argument from a Wealth of Material*: indicating that the speaker has many more good arguments or examples than he has time for.

*Climax*: placing the most important element in a series in final position.

*Commonplaces*: The places from which arguments can logically be drawn. This term originally meant the places of argument which are common to both sides of an argument. The term *topic* seems originally to have meant places from which arguments could be drawn, without reference to their being common to both sides. The two expressions were virtually synonymous by Aristotle's time. He uses *topic* almost exclusively. Some of his topics appear under "commonplaces" in Quintilian's *Institutio* and as "figures of diction" in the *Ad Herennium*.

*Concession*: admitting small points in order to give a tone of reasonableness without yielding a major point.

*Deference*: showing proper respect to opponents who deserve such respect or whom the speaker chooses to pretend deserve respect. This device is allied to concession, both being used as a part of the ethical proof.

*Deliberative Oratory*: one of the three kinds of speeches—that one used in the forum to debate future acts.

*Digression*: A set piece inserted between the Narration and the Proof in a speech, added to avoid tedium which might result from rushing into pugnacious argument after the Statement of Facts. The digression may contain anything within or without the case, just so it flows easily into the speech.

*Diminution*: using the lesser word or implying the lesser motive to a person or act.

*Direct Appeal to the Emotions*: usually an appeal to the fears, prejudice, pity, or self-interest of the audience.

*Elimination*: precluding all arguments or proposals or objections except the one being urged by the speaker.

*Epideictic Oratory*: one of the three kinds of speeches—that one concerned with praise or blame.

*Ethical Proof*: According to Aristotle (*Rhet.* I.ii.3.), there are three kinds of proof: ethical, emotional, and logical. The ethical stems from the moral character of the pleader himself: the audience is moved to acceptance through the moral force of a good man's speech.

*Exordium*: Because the connotation of the word *exordium* has come to indicate "an emotionally moving introduction," we in this century are likely to overlook any exordium which is not brilliantly moving and obvious in its intent. Quintilian, however, states that "the sole purpose of the exordium is to prepare the audience in such a way that they will be disposed to lend a ready ear to the rest of our speech." (*Instit.* IV.i.)

*Forensic Oratory*: one of the three kinds of speeches—that one used to determine guilt or innocence.

*Interrogation*: the speaker's posing a question which he immediately answers.

*Litotes*: verbal irony of understatement.

*Narration*: the second of the five parts of a speech, the part in which the facts are stated, or narrated.

*Ocular Demonstration*: sometimes called Vivid Picture; the speaker paints a "word-picture" of the thing of which he speaks.

*Peroration*: The fifth and final part of a speech, in which the speaker is free to use strong emotional appeal.

*Proof*: the third section of a speech, in which the logical proof of the proposition is argued.

*Proposition and Partition*: an optional part of a speech, inserted between the exordium and the narration, but after the digression (if one is used). The proposition is a concise statement of the contention or subject, followed by the partition, an outline of the several lines of proof under major headings.

*Refining*: dwelling on the same topic, yet seeming to say something new.

*Refutation*: the fourth section of a speech, in which the opponent's actual or anticipated objections are dealt with.

*Rhetorical Question*: a question so couched that only the answer desired by the speaker can reasonably be given.

*Sorites*: a formal argument based upon a long series of statements, each of which is logically connected only to the statements on each side: *a* is true, therefore *b* is true, therefore *c* is true, therefore *d* is true, etc. The result is that the first and last elements, no matter how apparently unrelated, are logically connected in this chain-like manner.

*Turning the Question*: the speaker manages to convict his opponent of the very charges made against the speaker.

# Index

Accumulation, 35, 113, 118, 138, 140, 146, 155
*Ad Herennium*, 29, 151 (n10, n14), 152(n2)
Amplification, 59-65, 86, 131, 132-35, 136, 138, 141-43, 155
Anticlimax, 83-84, 138, 145, 146, 155
Appeal to authority, 32-34, 42, 66-69, 86, 106-08, 117, 138, 143, 144, 155
Aristotle, 16, 34, 79, 138, 144, 150 (n1), 151(n12)

Cicero, 150(n3)
Concession, 18, 20-21, 35, 90-102, 116, 140, 155

Digression, 15, 17, 93-96, 156
Diminution, 22-29, 39, 41, 42, 51-59, 86, 102-05, 117, 129-32, 136, 138, 141-43, 156

Elimination, 35, 42, 111, 143, 156
Emotional oratory, 6-8, 9, 10, 12-13, 14, 15, 37-39, 42, 79-83, 86, 135-36, 138, 145, 146
Ethical proof, 16-22, 42, 45-51, 86, 88-102, 116, 121-29, 136, 138-41, 156
Exordium, 15, 16, 39, 46, 156

Interrogation, 34, 42, 156

*Journal to Stella*, 1, 13-14

Kilkenny School, 1, 149(n1)

*Letter to a Young Gentleman, Lately Enter'd Holy Orders*, 9-12
Litotes, 36-37, 39, 41, 42, 83, 112-13, 118, 138, 140, 145, 156

*New Journey to Paris, A* 14

Panegyric, 1, 2, 3
Parenthesis, 39-41, 42, 77-79, 108-11, 117-18, 145
Personification, 84-85, 86, 138, 145, 146, 147

Quintilian, 35, 149(n2), 150(n1, n3), 151(n6, n13), 152(n2, n6)

Refining, 29-32, 42, 138, 141, 157
Rhetorical curricula, 149(n1)
Rhetorical question, 69-77, 86, 111-12, 138, 145, 147, 157

*Tale of a Tub, A*, 1, 6-8
Trinity College, Dublin, 1
Turning the question, 108, 114-16, 140, 157

Wealth of argument, 40, 41, 138, 143